THE FAMILY CHURCH
Faith | Family | Fellowship

Rev. Dr. Roger A. Richardson
Foreword by Bishop Frederick Alan Wright, Sr.

Copyright © 2024 by Roger A. Richardson, Sr.

Published by RICHER Press
An Imprint of Richer Life, LLC

5710 Ogeechee Road, Suite 200-175, Savannah, Georgia 31405
www.richerlifellc.com

Cover Design: RICHER Media USA

Volume book discounts are available for groups, companies and organizations. Contact the publisher for information and order instructions.

No part of this publication may be reproduced, stored in a retrieval system, or transmitted in any form or by any means, electronic, mechanical, photocopying, recording, scanning, or otherwise, except as permitted under Section 107 or 108 of the 1976 United States Copyright Act, without prior written permission of the publisher.

The Family Church: Faith | Family | Fellowship

Rev. Dr. Roger A. Richardson

1. Religion 2. Inspiration 3. Educational
[pbk : alk. Paper]

Print Book: ISBN-13: 979-8-9863598-4-7
eBook: ISBN-13: 979-8-9863598-5-4

PRINTED IN THE UNITED STATES OF AMERICA

June 2024

ACKNOWLEDGEMENTS

The journey of *"The Family Church"* has been one of rediscovery, fueled by the collective spark of self-evaluation ignited by countless pastors, church members, and faithful patrons across the United States. To each of you, I offer my deepest gratitude. Your willingness to examine the concept of The Family Church from all angles, to hold it up to the light and rediscover its beauty and power, has been instrumental in shaping this book.

On a personal note, the man I am today would not be possible without the unwavering support of my family and friends. But my gratitude extends beyond them to the esteemed pastors under whose leadership I have served, observed, and grown as both a minister and a man. From them, I have learned the true essence of ministry. Therefore, it is with deep respect that I record their names within these pages: Reverend Dr. Cecil "Chip" Murray, Reverend Dr. Farrell Duncombe, Reverend Dr. W.E. Marshall, and Reverend Dr. Robert A. Strode.

Your guidance and mentorship have been invaluable gifts, shaping my understanding of faith and community.

Finally, I extend my heartfelt thanks to my wife, Joi Richardson, and my children, Naomi Richardson and Roger Richardson Jr. Their unwavering love and support have carried me through the many ups and downs of ministry. This book is a testament to their enduring strength and the incredible blessing they are in my life.

CONTENTS

FOREWORD
Bishop Frederick A. Wright, Sr.

PROLOGUE   11
Revival in Uncertain Times

INTRODUCTION   21
Pastor's Journey into the Heart of the Family Church

CHAPTER ONE   27
Rooted in the Vine
A Biblical Foundation for the Family Church

CHAPTER TWO   41
Unveiling the Two Faces of Family
A Theological Foundation for the Family Church

CHAPTER THREE   51
A Historical Foundation for the Family Church

CHAPTER FOUR   65
Building a Family Church – Ten Insights
A Journey of Connection and Growth

CHAPTER FIVE   93
A Case Study
Family Church Blossoms in a Mega Church Era

CHAPTER SIX
Transformational Sermons
More Than Memories: Rekindling the Family Church Vision
- ➢ *Keep the Fire Burning*   99
- ➢ *Living on Leftovers*   107

ABOUT THE AUTHOR   115

FOREWORD

When referring to the *church* there are several possible definitions. There is the *general* church, which includes all congregations of all religious faith and beliefs. There is the *local* church, whose constituents have a common faith and practice. There is the term *church* describing the worship service itself, such as *Let's have church*.

Rev. Dr. Roger A. Richardson, who served as a minister for over two decades invites us in his book to take a journey with him to explore the *church* as a *family church*. His inspiring vision in writing this book is to challenge the local small church to see the advantages she possesses to empower communities, cultivate deeper connections, nurture spiritual growth and serve as a beacon of hope for a changing world.

Dr. Richardson emphasizes how *Family Churches* offer a treasured intimacy that is unique, genuine and fulfilling. He establishes the thesis that a church uniqueness lies not in the size of the congregation but in the spirit and hearts of the congregation. *The Family Church* is the church where everyone knows our names. This familiarity of one another provides a special identity and connection that one is challenged to experience in mega churches. The book reveals how the unique spirit in the *Family Church* resonates deeply with a segment of population yearning for authentic connection, for genuine community and not as numbers listed on a spreadsheet, but as individuals woven into the fabric of something larger than themselves.

What I like about this book is the invitation to explore the hidden gems in the *Family Church* such as the unique strengths, the transformative power of intimacy, where belonging is not just a word but an actual experience that exists in the *Family Church*.

Therefore, would you join Dr. Richardson's exploration of the *Family Church* by reading the following pages before you, and discover the encouraging insights of the *Family Church*.

Bishop Frederick A. Wright, Sr.

Bishop Frederick Alan Wright, Sr. is the 142nd Bishop of the African Methodist Episcopal Church (AME). He was elected and consecrated in July 2021 and serves the 20th Episcopal District, which includes Malawi, Zimbabwe, and Uganda. Before becoming a bishop, Wright was the pastor of Quinn Chapel in Cincinnati, Ohio.

PROLOGUE

REVIVAL IN UNCERTAIN TIMES

Setting the Stage: A Sea of Change

We stand on the precipice of a new era, an era where the familiar ground beneath our feet feels like shifting sand. The anchors of community, family, and institutions that once held firm seem to be slowly giving way. While change has always been an inseparable thread in the human mosaic, the transformations swirling around us today carry a unique potency, a transformative weight unlike any before. It's not just the world around us that is in flux. We are in constant metamorphosis, ourselves, and caught in the ever-churning current of moral relativism and materialism.

Once, faith was a sturdy lighthouse, its beacon slicing through the darkest fog, guiding generations across uncharted waters. But the tide has turned, churning with a force unseen before. Hymnals gather dust, their melodies drowned out by the cacophony of a secular world. Pastors, once shepherds of light, grapple with the shadows of relevance, their voices barely audible above the din of a thousand competing philosophies.

Where are the pillars of strength, the voices that once thundered conviction, the hands that reached out with unwavering grace? Where is the sanctuary, the solace, the whisper of redemption in the storm's roar?

Challenges of the African American Community

Within this complex social landscape, the African American community faces a multitude of challenges. These challenges take the form of social issues that faith leaders and community organizations have consistently worked to address. Their focus is on identifying viable, fair-minded, and sustainable solutions.

Here are just a few of the most glaring challenges within this paralyzing puzzle.

Widening Economic Disparities.

A recent 2023 Pew Research Center study [see chart below] reveals a staggering wealth gap, with the median white family holding ten times the wealth of the median Black family. This disparity translates into limited opportunities, stifled dreams, and a constant struggle for stability.

Impact of Wealth Allocations on the Median Black-White Wealth Disparity, By Policy

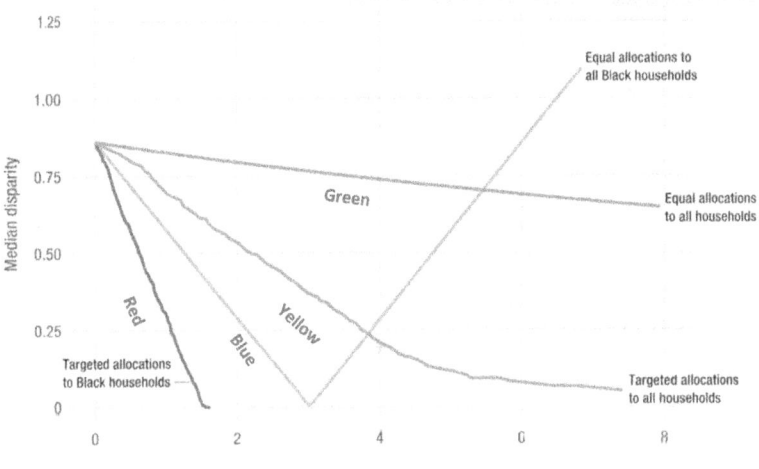

This chart shows how Black-White wealth disparities would change under four scenarios the researchers considered. The blue line shows equal allocations to all Black households, a scenario most similar to proposed reparations policies. It would reduce the median disparity to zero at $3 trillion; allocations beyond that would reverse the disparity, as shown in the chart. The red line shows a more-targeted allocation to Black households based on need. The yellow and green lines show allocations to all households, regardless of race. One example would be baby bonds given to all newborn children (or targeted to all children below a certain wealth threshold).

Source: May 9, 2023, ESSAY: *What Would It Take to Close America's Black-White Wealth Gap?* The RAND Research Organization.

Family Structure.

The lack of robust support networks leaves many families teetering on the edge. In 2021, the Brookings Institution reported that 61% of Black children were raised in households by a single parent, compared to 20% of white children. This absence of a two-parent structure often leads to increased poverty, lower educational attainment, and higher incidences of behavioral problems.

Political Disenfranchisement.

The feeling of limited influence over governing institutions festers. A 2022 Brennan Center for Justice report found that Black voters face a disproportionate share of voting restrictions, with states adopting measures like voter ID laws and reduced polling locations that hinder their ability to exercise their fundamental right.

Social Media's Grip.

Social Media's pervasive influence, across all ages, poses significant emotional challenges. A 2020 Kaiser Family Foundation study found that Black teens spend significantly more time on social media than their white counterparts, exacerbating anxieties and depression, particularly among girls.

Educational Hurdles.

Affordability, access, and the quality of education remain significant barriers. A 2022 Education Trust report revealed that Black students are 3.5 times more likely than white students to attend underfunded schools, perpetuating a deep and continuing cycle of educational disadvantage.

Housing Injustices.

Systemic biases still continue to haunt and plague financing, appraisals and ownership. For example, a 2021 Urban Institute study found that Black homeowners are denied mortgages at a rate two times higher than white homeowners, even when controlling for factors such as family income and credit score.

Family Fragmentation.

Divorce, single parenthood, and grandparent-led households are on the rise. A 2023 Census Bureau report showed that 64% of Black children have lived in a single-parent household at some point in their lives, compared to 28% of white children. This instability can negatively impact children's emotional well-being, and academic performance.

Moral Shifts.

Moral shifts fueled by consumerism, materialism, and secularism threaten community cohesion and breed individualism. A 2022 Pew Research Center survey found that only 45% of Black adults identify as religiously affiliated, down from 84% in 1990. This decline in religious participation can weaken social bonds and erode a sense of shared purpose.

The Church at the Crossroads

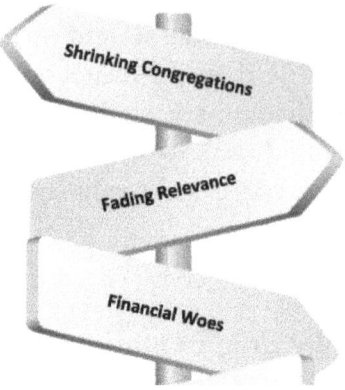

Amidst these challenges, the church, once a haven and a pillar of the African American community, finds itself at a crossroads. The statistics paint a stark picture of its decline. Here are some of the driving factors.

Shrinking Congregations.

Carey Nieuwhof's research shows that the median congregation size in the United States has shrunk dramatically, from 135 in 2000 to just 60 in 2023. Online attendance does offer a slight bump, but the downward trend is undeniable.

Fading Relevance.

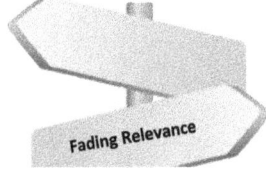

A 2022 Gallup poll found that only 72% of Americans with a religious affiliation belong to a church, down from 79% in 1998-2000. This most significant decline is particularly pronounced among younger generations, with only 27% of Gen Z identifying as religiously affiliated compared to 56% of Boomers (Pew Research Center).

Financial Woes.

A 2023 National Council of Churches report revealed that unbelievably one in five U.S. churches are seriously facing financial difficulty, struggling to keep their doors open. This financial instability hinders their ability to serve their communities and fund vital programs.

The Call for Revival

This is the crucible in which we, as African American pastors, and community leaders, find ourselves. We strive to strengthen a community besieged by challenges while simultaneously reviving an institution facing its own existential crisis. The data on church decline, especially acute within the African American community, paints a grim picture. Regardless of the denomination or the location, church attendance, resources, participation and capacity have plummeted.

We stand at a crossroads, an institution besieged by obstacles yet desperately clinging to relevance. In the face of such daunting odds, one could easily succumb to despair.

But like Isaiah, we gaze upon the barren landscape, envisioning what could be, asking ourselves: *"Can these bones live again?"*

I believe the answer to this question is "yes." Here are three actions that could lead the way.

1. Rekindle the Fire.

Revival is our only hope for lasting relevance and survival. We need a fresh wave of the Holy Spirit, an anointing that transforms us into fearless champions of the Gospel, eternal optimists, and unwavering advocates for God's transformative power. This revival won't come through ignoring our current realities. It demands bold preaching, inspiring teaching, and a call to action that compels our members to offer God their best service.

2. Reconnect with Community.

Revival necessitates the reconnecting with the communities we serve. We must tailor our programs and ministries to address their specific spiritual and temporal needs. The church must be a beacon of love, peace, integrity, and safety – a place where souls can find solace and work out their salvation.

3. Revitalize our Facilities.

We must revitalize our physical spaces, transforming them into welcoming, functional, and inspiring sanctuaries that beckon people in – not just on Sundays, but throughout the week. Most of the Black community today experiences vibrant architecture and welcoming spaces in all walks of their life. They yearn to worship in environments that mirror their dedication to progress and their pursuit of personal and spiritual fulfillment. To welcome a new generation of faith, we must revitalize our facilities. Not just as houses of worship, but as hubs of fellowship, engagement, and accessibility built for the ministry of today.

This book is my attempt to offer answers and perspectives on ministry, gleaned from my journeys as an itinerant preacher. It's not a definitive solution, but rather an invitation to re-examine what it means to do ministry. Whether pastor or layperson, we are all engaged in this sacred work. Our understanding of ourselves and the church's purpose will determine how we approach this task.

My hope is that this book will spark a self-evaluation, prompting us to redefine who we are and what we offer to the communities we serve. The more we engage in this dialogue, both locally and beyond, the better equipped we'll be to foster the change we desire and bring about a true revival.

Together, let us rise to the challenges, rekindle the flames of faith, and watch the bones live again.

"The strength of connection forged in intimate spaces, the beauty of a community where belonging takes precedence over spectacle is powerful in and of itself."

INTRODUCTION

PASTOR'S JOURNEY INTO THE HEART OF THE FAMILY CHURCH

The catalyst for this book, the foundation of my ministry, isn't etched in stone or enshrined in a grand theological treatise. It emerges from a seemingly simple conversation, a casual remark from my mentor, a man who shepherded a fledgling church into a beacon within our denomination. As we discussed our ministries, sharing the triumphs and tribulations of life in the pulpit, his words landed with a surprising weight: *"You pastor a family church."*

Initially, a tinge of confusion clouded my mind. Was this an offhand comment, or casual observation? Or perhaps, was somewhere, nestled within those syllables, lurked a subtle critique, and a gentle nudge towards loftier ambitions? My mentor, however, was far removed from the realm and depth of veiled pronouncements. Our bond, forged in years of shared laughter and theological wrestling, assured me his words emanated from a pure source – a keen eye for the essence of things.

Days, then weeks, then months unfolded, and his statement continued to resonate within me. Had I, in my quest for growth, strayed from the fundamental nature of this place I served? Was this label, *Family Church*, a badge of limitation or a hidden gem waiting to be unearthed? This seemingly incidental remark became a koan, a constant meditation that nudged me towards a deeper understanding of ministry, my congregation, and ultimately, myself.

To truly grasp the power of this revelation, we must first navigate the murky waters of classification. Researchers, ever eager to quantify spiritual experience, have devised various systems to categorize churches based on size. The National Council of Churches, while lacking a universal system, might label yours as "large" if a thousand souls grace your pews, "medium" if a few hundred gather, and "small" if your community hums with less than two hundred and fifty. Others, like Hartford Institute for Religion Research, paint broader strokes, defining megachurches by the thousands they draw, large churches by the hundreds, and medium churches by the tens.

However, as I delved into these classifications, a curious reality began to glimmer. Regardless of the chosen yardstick, most churches in the US fall within the medium to small range. The Hartford Institute reports that over 90% of Protestant churches boast less than 500 attendees, while Lifeway Research, in their insightful 2020 FACT study, reveals that a staggering seven out of ten U.S. churches see less than a hundred souls gather for weekly worship. These statistics painted a different picture, one where *family church* wasn't the exception but was the rule.

This concept of *Family Church* wasn't merely a size designation, but a vision of something deeper, a murmur of intimacy that transcended numbers. Arlin Rothauge, another voice in this ongoing conversation, offered a fascinating perspective. He argued that program success depended on the unique dynamics of each congregation, and the most potent predictor of these dynamics is *size*. His primary focus, as I understood it, lay in uncovering the intricate dance between a church's character and its interaction with both its members and the broader community. Rothauge, while using similar size descriptors, primarily concerned himself with the connection between size and operation. He contended that churches of certain sizes offered distinct experiences, catering to specific needs within the greater community, their programming shaped by their very stature.

Yet, as I dug deeper, another truth emerged. *Family Church* wasn't a neatly defined box, but a kaleidoscope of interpretations. It could shimmer with the promise of programs tailored to children, their laughter echoing through the halls. Or it could pulse with the warmth of intergenerational connection, where grandparents and grandchildren sat shoulder to shoulder, reciting stories and sharing faith. For some, it embodied the spirit of their denomination, the values and structures passed down through generations, finding fertile ground in this intimate setting. And for others, it might simply be a matter of size – a cozy haven compared to sprawling megachurches, a place where faces were familiar and greetings were personal.

This inherent ambiguity, I realized, wasn't a weakness, but a strength. It allowed for churches of all shapes and sizes to embrace the essence of "family" without being confined by rigid definitions. It offered a space for the organic flourishing of community, where connections blossomed not from forced programs or imposed structures, but from the fertile ground of shared faith and genuine human connection.

However, within this ambiguity lurked a danger. As long as a disconnect existed between our perception of ourselves and who we truly were, we risked losing sight of our unique strengths, our inherent value. When a family church yearns to mimic the megachurch, it unwittingly abandons the intimate, venturing into a space it's neither equipped for nor meant to occupy. This pursuit of bigness often overlooks the quiet power of smallness, the strength of connection forged in intimate spaces, the beauty of a community where belonging takes precedence.

The **strength of connection** forged in intimate spaces, the beauty of a community where belonging takes precedence over spectacle is powerful in and of itself. It's like neglecting a delicate wildflower garden for the allure of a manicured lawn, sacrificing the vibrant, diverse ecosystem for a uniform expanse of green. Instead, embracing **our role** as family churches requires a radical shift in perspective, a conscious decision to celebrate the unique offerings we bring to the world of faith.

Our **strength lies not in numbers, but in intimacy.** Imagine a bustling marketplace, each stall overflowing with goods. Megachurches are the glittering department stores, offering dazzling displays and a vast array of choices. Family churches, in contrast, are the quaint, tucked-away shops, specializing in handcrafted wares and personalized service. We don't offer the sheer volume of the mass-produced, but the warmth of the hand stitched. Within our walls, names are remembered, stories are shared, and burdens are lifted, one soul at a time. We prioritize depth over breadth, fostering bonds that go beyond Sunday greetings, extending into shared meals, communal prayers, and a constant presence in times of need.

Our value lies not in programs, but in presence. The allure of big-box ministry often lies in its organized efficiency, its streamlined programs catering to every conceivable need. Family churches, however, offer a different kind of value. We prioritize presence over programming, recognizing that the most transformative moments often arise not from scripted activities, but from the spontaneous encounters, the shared laughter over coffee, the quiet words of comfort offered between pews. In our smaller communities, the pastor isn't just a distant figure on a stage, but a familiar face, a shepherd who knows his flock, tending to their individual needs with patient attentiveness.

Our uniqueness lies not in size, but in spirit. Size may be a convenient metric, but it fails to capture the essence of a family church. At our core, we are not defined by the number of chairs in our sanctuary, but by the shared spirit that animates them. We are the church where everyone knows your name, where the door is always open, and where a helping hand is never far away. We are the church where children's laughter mingles with the wisdom of elders, where tears are not judged, and where vulnerability finds a safe haven. We are the church where faith isn't merely professed, but embodied in everyday acts of kindness, compassion, and service.

This unique spirit resonates deeply with a segment of the population yearning for authentic connection, for genuine community, for a place where they are seen and heard, not as numbers on a spreadsheet, but as individuals woven into the fabric of something larger than themselves. This is the niche family churches excel in, the space where we have a competitive advantage, the market we are uniquely positioned to serve.

However, embracing this calling requires a *paradigm shift* not just for congregations, but for pastors as well. In an age where success is often measured in celebrity status and megachurch empires, can we, as shepherds of smaller flocks, find fulfillment in tending to our intimate gardens? Can we redefine our own notions of success, finding value not in the applause of crowds, but in the quiet displays of gratitude, the steady growth of faith within our communities, the transformative impact on individual lives? Can we draw our self-worth not from the size of our budget or the breadth of our programs, but from the depth of our connections, the authenticity of our presence, and the transformative power of the gospel lived out in everyday moments?

This is the challenge and the privilege of leading a family church. It is not a path for the faint of heart, but it is a path brimming with meaning, purpose, and an unparalleled potential for impact. It is a call to cultivate fertile ground for genuine community, to celebrate the quiet power of intimacy, and to offer a haven of belonging in a world often defined by isolation and anonymity.

This book is an invitation to explore this calling, to delve into the heart of the family church, to uncover its hidden gems, and to challenge the misconceptions that hold it back. Together, we will discover the unique strengths that lie dormant within our walls, the transformative power of intimacy, and the profound fulfillment that comes from building a community where belonging is not just a word, but a lived experience.

So, join me on this journey. Let us hold the concept of the family church up to the light, examine its facets, and rediscover the beauty and power that lie within. Let us celebrate the strength of smallness, the magic of connection, and the transformative potential of a community bound by faith, love, and the shared journey of belonging.

CHAPTER ONE

ROOTED IN THE VINE
A Biblical Foundation for the Family Church

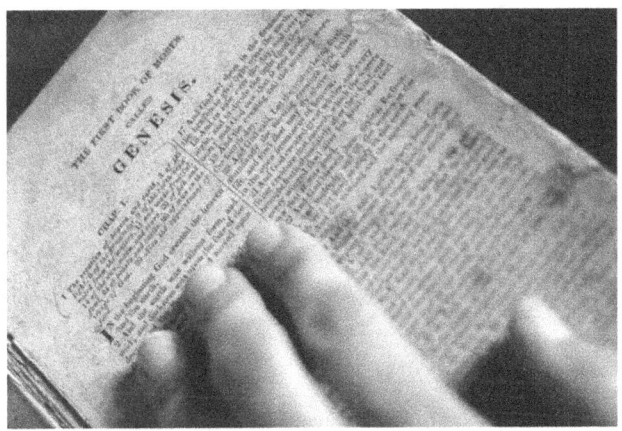

In the quiet moments of reflection, as my understanding of the family church deepened, I yearned for a compass, a guiding light amidst the evolving landscape of faith. Surely, within the vast expanse of scripture, filled with wisdom and divine love, there would be evidence of what it truly meant to be a family church – a haven of intimate connection, where souls shared in profound spiritual experiences and embarked on a collective journey illuminated by a shared view of God. It might seem, to the casual observer, a concept born of our modern times, a response to the shifting sands of belief.

Yet, the seeds of this familial expression of Christian community lie dormant, waiting to be unearthed, in the fertile soil of scripture. Embarking on this journey through ancient texts, like eager explorers traversing a map etched with love and divine truths, we seek not just answers, but wisdom – gleaned from the stories of lives transformed, the echoes of teachings that still resonate across millennia. For it is in this fertile ground, nourished by the living water of God's word, that we discover the roots of the family church, strong and enduring, ready to blossom into a haven of belonging, growth, and shared purpose for those who seek a faith woven with the threads of kinship and love.

ROOTED IN UNITY: BEYOND BLOODLINES TO SHARED HEARTS

As we navigate the landscape of the family church, one figure stands as our guiding light – Jesus, the embodiment of love who redefined the very concept of family. In John 17:20-23, his words resonate with a transformative power:

"My prayer is not for them alone. I pray also for those who will believe in me through their message, that they may all be one. Father, just as you are in me and I am in you, may they also be in us so that the world may believe that you sent me. I have given them the glory that you gave me, that they may be one as we are one – I in them and you in me – so that they may be brought to perfect unity. Then the world will know that you sent me and loved them as you loved me."

Here, Jesus envisions a unity that transcends earthly ties, a spiritual experience of shared faith and divine love. This radical notion echoes throughout his teachings, as demonstrated in Mark 3:31-35:

"Then Jesus' mother and brothers arrived. Standing outside, they sent someone to ask him to come out to them. 'Your mother and brothers are here outside,' the messenger told him. He replied, 'Who are my mother and brothers?' Looking at those seated around him, he said, 'Here are my mother and brothers! Whoever does God's will is my brother and sister and mother.'"

Jesus doesn't dismantle the importance of biological families, but expands its definition to include those who share a commitment to God's will. This radical inclusivity becomes the cornerstone of the family church, where bloodlines recede, making way for a haven of belonging forged in shared faith and love.

Within this vibrant community, individuals find themselves woven into a fabric of kinship that transcends earthly bonds. Strangers become brothers and sisters, united by a common calling and a shared journey towards Christ. Support and encouragement flow freely, nurtured by the deep understanding that arises from walking a similar path. Growth and transformation become collective endeavors, as individuals learn and grow from each other's experiences, their unique gifts and talents enriching the whole. This isn't merely an idyllic dream, but a lived reality within the family church. Witness the tears shared in mourning, the joys celebrated in triumphs, the burdens lightened through shared prayers, and the laughter that echoes through moments of fellowship. Each experience strengthens the bonds of unity, creating a haven where hearts find home amidst a community defined not by blood, but by a shared love for God and one another.

In this light, the family church emerges as a powerful testament to Jesus's radical vision of unity. It challenges us to look beyond the surface, to embrace the notion that our true family transcends earthly ties, encompassing all who share the flame of faith in their hearts. Here, we discover that belonging isn't about bloodlines, but about the shared language of love that flows from soul to soul.

BLUEPRINT FOR CHRISTIAN UNITY

But this familial bond isn't merely sentimental. It translates into action, guided by the principles laid out in Scripture. Ephesians 4:1-6 (NLT) beautifully outlines the blueprint for living in unity:

"As a prisoner for the Lord, then, I urge you to live a life worthy of the calling you have received. Be completely humble and gentle; be patient, bearing one another in love. Make every effort to keep the unity of the Spirit through the bond of peace. For there is one body and one Spirit, just as you were called to one hope when you were called. One Lord, one faith, one baptism, one God and Father of all, who is over all and through all and in all."

This passage lays bare the foundation for genuine Christian community. Humility, gentleness, patience, love, and unity, bound together by the "bond of peace," the very peace offered by Christ himself. Within the family church, this isn't merely an aspiration, but a lived reality. Members strive to embody these virtues, creating a safe space where vulnerability blooms, honest communication flourishes, and disagreements are handled with grace and mutual respect.

DIVERSITY WITHIN UNITY: THE CALL FOR TOGETHERNESS

The emphasis on unity doesn't stifle individuality, but encourages its flourishing. In 1 Corinthians 12:7-11 (NLT), Paul celebrates the diversity of gifts within the body of Christ, stating:

"To each is given the manifestation of the Spirit for the common good. To one there is given the word of wisdom through the Spirit, to another the word of knowledge by the same Spirit, to another faith by the same Spirit, to another

gifts of healing by the same Spirit, to another miraculous powers, to another prophecy, to another distinguishing between spirits, to another various kinds of tongues, to another the interpretation of tongues. All these are the work of one and the same Spirit, and he distributes them to each one just as he determines."

Just as a healthy family thrives on the unique contributions of its members, so too does the family church. Musicians ignite worship with their melodies, teachers nurture understanding with their insights, and encouragers uplift spirits with their kind words. These diverse gifts, guided by the Holy Spirit, work in concert to build a vibrant community where each member feels valued and empowered to contribute.

GATHERED IN HIS PRESENCE: WHERE LIFE'S MILESTONES BECOME MIRACLES

Christ's first miracle wasn't a grand spectacle, but a quiet blessing at a wedding feast. Let's revisit John 2:1-3 (NLT):

"On the third day there was a wedding celebration in the village of Cana in Galilee. Jesus' mother was there, 2 and Jesus and his disciples were also invited to the celebration. 3 The wine supply ran out during the festivities, so Jesus' mother told him, They have no more wine."

In these verses, a seemingly mundane event – a wedding celebration running short on wine – sets the stage for a momentous act. Notice how subtly Jesus enters the scene, invited amidst family and friends. His first miracle isn't performed on a grand platform, but within the ordinary occurrences of life, amidst laughter and celebration. This deliberate setting holds a profound truth: God's miracles unfold not just in dramatic pronouncements, but in the very fabric of our lives, especially when woven with threads of faith and shared joy.

The family church embraces this truth, becoming a haven where life's moments, big and small, are intertwined into a sacred symphony. Here, marriages are blessed, vows recited in the presence of loved ones, a family united under the banner of faith. Baptism becomes a joyous initiation, welcoming newborns into the embrace of God's community. Birthdays bloom with laughter and shared memories, reminding us of the gift of life itself. Anniversaries recall tales of love's endurance, a testament to the power of commitment. Retirements mark the culmination of dedicated work, celebrated with gratitude and well wishes. Graduations become beacons of hope, launching young lives into the world with the blessings of community. Baby showers echo with anticipation, as a new life prepares to join the community of faith.

In each gathering, a miracle unfolds. Not always a spectacle, but a subtle dance of God's grace woven into the fabric of our lives. Laughter shared strengthens bonds, stories exchanged deepen understanding, and tears shed together bind hearts in empathy. These seemingly ordinary moments become mosaics of divine intervention, drawing us closer to one another and to God.

The family church is the canvas upon which these miracles are painted. It's the gathering place where life's celebrations resonate with faith, where milestones become steppingstones on our shared journey. Here, we find solace in knowing that God isn't confined to sanctuaries, but dwells amidst the joyous clamor of life, bestowing blessings in the rustle of laughter and etching miracles in the shared moments of our human experience.

THE POWER OF INTIMACY: SMALL FLAMES, MIGHTY FIRES

While visions of bustling mega-churches often dance in our minds when we contemplate the church, Acts 1 paints a different picture. The foundation of the New Testament church wasn't laid in a spectacular arena, but in the humble confines of an upper room, amongst a mere 120 believers (Acts 1:15). These verses, Acts 1:12-15 (NLT), reveal the potency of small communities gathered in faith:

> *"Then the apostles returned to Jerusalem from the Mount of Olives, a distance of half a mile. 13 When they arrived, they went to the upstairs room of the house where they were staying. Here are the names of those who were present: Peter, John, James, Andrew, Philip, Thomas, Bartholomew, Matthew, James (son of Alphaeus), Simon (the zealot), and Judas (son of James). 14 They all met together and were constantly united in prayer, along with Mary the mother of Jesus, several other women, and the brothers of Jesus. 15 During this time, when about 120 believers were together in one place, Peter stood up and addressed them."*

Notice the emphasis on unity and shared purpose in this passage. These believers weren't a scattered assembly, but *"constantly united in prayer,"* their hearts united together in a symphony of faith. Though small in number, they possessed a spiritual might that would ignite a global movement.

The family church embodies this very essence. It's a haven where quantity yields to quality, where deep connections forge bonds of support and encouragement. Within these intimate gatherings, individuals aren't lost in a sea of faces, but embraced as integral threads in the fabric of community. This environment fosters genuine vulnerability, open communication, and a shared journey of spiritual growth.

Remember the early church in Acts? Despite their limited numbers, they experienced pivotal moments; choosing Matthias to replace Judas, receiving the Holy Spirit, and embarking on the monumental task of spreading the gospel. It was their unwavering faith, fueled by the intimacy of their communal bond, which empowered them to achieve seemingly insurmountable goals.

The family church holds this same potential. Through shared moments of worship, study, and service, believers become partners in a collective mission. Each individual's gifts and talents find fertile ground to flourish, contributing to the collective strength and vitality of the community. In this fertile ground, small flames of faith blossom into mighty fires, illuminating the path for others and leaving a lasting impact on the world around them.

So, while the allure of large crowds may be undeniable, let us not underestimate the power of intimacy. The family church, with its focus on deep connection and shared purpose, offers a powerful alternative – a space where small groups of believers, united in faith and love, can become catalysts for transformative change.

Weaving Harmony: The Threads of Unity

While the concept of Christian unity often evokes grand gatherings and unified voices, Scripture reveals a blueprint crafted in more intimate spaces. Ephesians 4:1-6 (NLT) offers a poignant reminder:

"As a prisoner for the Lord, then, I urge you to live a life worthy of the calling you have received. Be completely humble and gentle; be patient, bearing with one another in love. Make every effort to keep the unity of the Spirit through the bond of peace. For there is one body and one Spirit, just as you were called to one hope when you were called; one Lord, one faith, one baptism; one God and Father of all, who is over all and through all and in all."

Within these verses, we discover the foundation for genuine Christian community, woven not from grand gestures but from the threads of humility, gentleness, patience, and love. The binding force is the *"bond of peace,"* a peace born of Christ himself.

The *Family Church* embraces this blueprint, embodying unity not as a lofty aspiration but as a lived reality. In these intimate gatherings, members strive to embody these virtues, creating a sacred space where vulnerability can bloom, honest communication can flourish, and disagreements are handled with grace and mutual respect.

Imagine a circle of believers, gathered not in a vast cathedral but in the warmth of a living room. Their voices mingle in prayer, their hearts open to one another's joys and sorrows. Here, humility finds fertile ground, as individuals seek to learn from one another, prioritizing the well-being of the community over personal agendas. Gentleness softens potential conflicts, while patience allows for diverse perspectives and voices to be heard. And love, that most profound of virtues, forms the bedrock, binding hearts together in a shared journey of faith.

This is the essence of unity in the family church — not a uniformity that erases individuality, but a harmonious symphony where each voice contributes its unique melody, guided by the shared rhythm of Christ's love. It's a testament to the power of intimacy, where deep connections forge bonds that can weather storms and celebrate triumphs, fostering a resilience that transcends individual challenges.

EMBRACING ABUNDANCE: SHARING AS AN ACT OF FAITH

While towering steeple and grand choirs often paint the picture of the church, Acts 2 reveals a different narrative — one forged in intimate gatherings and deep concern for one another's well-being. These verses, Acts 2:42-47 (NLT), offer a glimpse into the heart of the early church:

"All the believers devoted themselves to the apostles' teaching, and to fellowship, and to sharing in meals (including the Lord's Supper), and to prayer. A deep sense of awe came over them all, and the apostles performed many miraculous signs and wonders. And all the believers met together in one place and shared everything they had. They sold their property and possessions and shared the money with those in need. They worshiped together at the Temple each day, met in homes for the Lord's Supper, and shared their meals with great joy and generosity — all the while praising God and enjoying the goodwill of all the people. And each day the Lord added to their fellowship those who were being saved."

Notice the emphasis on shared abundance. This wasn't a community content with merely spiritual nourishment; it actively prioritized the temporal well-being of its members. Financial needs were not met with distant pronouncements, but with outstretched hands and open hearts. Homes became more than abodes; they were sanctuaries of shared laughter and support, where burdens were lightened and hope was celebrated.

The *Family Church* carries this torch, embodying the spirit of abundance in practical ways. Members open their homes, offering refuge to those navigating homelessness or loneliness. Financial resources are pooled, creating a safety net of support for seniors and families weathering tough times. This radical generosity isn't merely altruistic; it's an expression of faith lived out. Sharing isn't about emptying pockets, but about recognizing the abundance that flows from God's grace. When one member struggles, the entire body feels the ache, and compassion becomes the guiding force. This outward display of love, woven into the fabric of everyday life, becomes a beacon of hope for those seeking a haven of genuine care.

Remember, the early church didn't simply attract; it radiated. Their shared joys and open hearts, fueled by practical acts of support, drew in those yearning for a space of belonging. The family church embraces this same potential. By prioritizing the well-being of its members, creating a safety net of shared resources and unwavering compassion, it becomes a sanctuary for the weary, a testament to the transformative power of love that extends beyond the pulpit.

A CHORUS OF APPRECIATION: CELEBRATING EVERY VOICE

While grand choirs often dominate the soundscape of a church, Romans 12:10 (NLT) offers a different melody: *"Love each other with genuine affection, and take delight in honoring one another."* This verse, resonating within the family church, becomes a harmonious song celebrating not just star soloists, but every voice — every individual — contributing to the joyful chorus of community.

> ➤ **Notice the Shift from Solo Spotlights to Shared Applause**

The early church wasn't content with recognizing only a chosen few; it actively cherished the unique contributions of all its members. Gathering wasn't just about collective worship; it was a vibrant orchestra where every instrument, regardless of tone or volume, was valued for its role in the beautiful composition.

> ➤ **The Family Church Echoes this Symphony in Practical Ways**

Schedule special days for different groups — children, seniors, men, and women. This will offer a stage for appreciation. Heartfelt acknowledgements during services weave a melody of gratitude into the fabric of community life. Spontaneous expressions of support in daily interactions ensure that no contribution goes unheard.

> ➤ **This Culture of Celebration isn't Mere Background Noise**

It's a vital harmony in the family church's song. When individuals feel seen, valued, and celebrated for their unique gifts, their spirits soar. A sense of belonging takes root, deepening their commitment to the shared journey of faith and service. The joy of recognition becomes a catalyst, fueling individual growth and inspiring others to pick up their own instruments and add their voices to the collective song.

By prioritizing the recognition of all its members, it becomes a vibrant testament to the transformative power of love that extends beyond grand gestures and into the hearts of every individual. It's a testament to the power of connection, where deep relationships form the chords that bind individuals together, creating a space where every voice feels valued, empowered, and woven into the beautiful composition of the family church.

EMBRACING PRESENCE: MAKING LOVE TANGIBLE

While vaulted ceilings often pierce the sky, John 13:34-35 (NLT) elucidates a different truth: *"So now I am giving you a new commandment: Love each other. Just as I have loved you, you should love each other. Your love for one another will prove to the world that you are my disciples."* This verse, etched in the heart of the family church, becomes a lens through which we see and engage the world—a lens focused not on grand pronouncements, but on the transformative power of presence, of making love tangible through shared moments and experiences.

Notice the shift from words to action. John's commandment isn't about mere sentiment; it's a call to embody love, to infuse it into the fabric of everyday life. The family church echoes this call, not with distant pronouncements, but with open arms and shared tables.

Here, love is made flesh in the breaking of bread, the laughter in homes, the tears in times of hardship, and the shared joys of celebrations. It unfolds in the quiet hours of conversation, the whispered prayers of support, and the helping hands that lighten burdens. In the family church, the most precious resource—time—is readily shared, an offering of connection and a testament to the depth of love that binds the community together.

This wasn't a new concept for Christ's disciples. They followed a master who walked among them, ate with them, and entered the ordinary spaces of their lives. His love wasn't an abstract ideal; it was intertwined in the fabric of their days, a constant thread of presence and support.

The family church embraces this same ethos. Through shared meals, gatherings, and moments of fellowship, it creates a space where love is made tangible, where memories are built, and where relationships flourish in the fertile ground of shared experiences. Here, the bonds of community become a living testament to Christ's example, a beacon of hope that radiates outward, inviting others to experience the transformative power of love embodied in daily life.

This is the essence of presence in the family church — not a fleeting glance or a distant pronouncement, but a deep, abiding connection fueled by the constant sharing of time, joy, and hardship. It's a testament to the power of Christ's love, not as a lofty ideal, but as a shared journey where every member feels seen and valued. It's in these seemingly ordinary moments, in the laughter, the tears, and the shared bread, that love finds its truest expression, transforming lives and radiating hope into the world, one precious moment at a time.

CHAPTER TWO

UNVEILING THE TWO FACES OF FAMILY
A Theological Foundation for the Family Church

Behind the elaborate altars and stained-glass windows of the church lies a hidden crossroads, where the concept of "family" takes on intriguing complexities within the realm of faith. Though the terms *"family church"* and *"family ministry"* often dance hand-in-hand, their theological underpinnings hold distinct nuances, like two sides of the same coin revealing faces sculpted by different hands. This chapter embarks on a quest to unveil these nuanced perspectives, dissecting their inherent strengths and limitations, ultimately unveiling their unique roles in cultivating faith and fostering community within the church walls.

On the one hand, we encounter the "family ministry" approach, its gaze firmly fixed on the fundamental unit – the nuclear family. Imagine a nurturing garden bathed in sunlight, where parents, the dedicated gardeners, lovingly tend the tender shoots of their children's faith. Proverbs 22:6 echoes in this setting, *"Direct your children onto the right path, and when they are older, they will not leave it."* Here, equipping parents with resources and tools like family devotionals, age-appropriate Bible studies, and strategies for weaving faith into daily routines becomes the cornerstone. The ideal is a home transformed into a vibrant place of faith, where mealtimes hum with grace, chores morph into lessons in service, and even mundane tasks resonate with the quiet murmur of prayer.

But this idyllic scene faces the stark reality of contemporary landscapes. Single-parent households, blended families, and non-traditional structures blur the lines of the *"nuclear"* image. Family ministry, then, must shed the rigidity of a walled garden and embrace the open, dynamic expanse of a thriving forest. Flexible resources, inclusive programs, and sensitive pastoral care become paramount. This approach celebrates the inherent strength and wisdom within each family unit, empowering parents, regardless of structure, to become the primary spiritual influencers in their children's lives. It fosters not just individual faith in young hearts, but also a shared journey of faith within the family constellation, where parents and children navigate the terrain of belief together, each branch supporting the other as they reach for the sun.

Yet, across the path stands another vision, its gaze sweeping beyond the boundaries of blood ties and familial structures. Here, the "family church" emerges, its arms outstretched in a warm embrace that gathers individuals of all ages, backgrounds, and experiences into a haven of shared faith. It echoes the sentiment of John 13:34-35, where Jesus proclaims, *"A new commandment I give you: Love one another. As I have loved you, so you must love one another. By this all will know that you are my disciples, if you have love for one another."*

This verse becomes the guiding light, illuminating a community where *"woman, behold your son"* transcends Calvary and resonates within the very pulse of the church family.

This vision unfolds in bright and vibrant hues. Shared worship experiences become kaleidoscopes of many generations, with grandparents singing alongside grandchildren and teenagers finding kindred spirits in spirited youth groups. Sunday school transforms into a bustling marketplace of faith, where young minds explore Bible stories while adults delve deeper into scripture in dedicated studies. Mentors emerge from within the community, not just parents but experienced members offering guidance and support, becoming spiritual anchors for those seeking a secure harbor.

But the embrace of the family church extends beyond doctrinal teachings. It weaves practical threads of support into its very fabric. Crisis counseling and emergency assistance stand ready to catch those facing unexpected storms, their compassion a safety net woven from the collective strength of the community. Meals are shared, childcare offered, and burdens lifted, as church members embody the hands and feet of Jesus, demonstrating love through tangible acts of kindness.

Thus, we stand at this crossroads, where the paths of family ministry and family church diverge, each beckoning with its unique promise. To fully grasp their potential, we must delve deeper, exploring the intricate details of their approaches, strengths, and challenges. This journey demands careful thought and discerning eyes, for within these nuanced theologies lies the power to unlock a ministry of community within the church, where every individual, regardless of their family landscape, can find a cherished place at the table of grace.

❖ PART 1: A THEOLOGY OF FAMILY MINISTRY

The Nuclear Family as the Crucible: Cultivating Faith within the Home Garden

Imagine a fertile garden basking under the sun, where dedicated parents lovingly tend the sprouts of their children's faith. This idyllic image captures the essence of family ministry theology, which places the nuclear family at the heart of spiritual growth. Parents, armed with tools for family worship, Bible study, and faith-filled conversations, become the primary cultivators of their children's inner landscapes. Scriptures like Proverbs 22:6 become their guiding light, *"Direct your children onto the right path, and when they are older, they will not leave it."*

This approach resonates with Tony Dungy's sentiment, *"The family is the foundational institution of society, and when it is strong, the entire community thrives."* Family ministry seeks to empower families, transforming them into the bedrock of a robust spiritual community. This vision rests on the belief that within the intimate space of the family, faith takes root and flourishes, nourished by love, trust, and shared experiences.

The strengths of this approach lie in its focus on parental agency. Family ministry equips parents, regardless of their family structure, to be the primary spiritual influencers in their children's lives. It celebrates the inherent wisdom and strength within each family unit, encouraging parents to draw and act upon their unique thoughts, experiences and relationships to create a vibrant home environment where faith permeates every facet of daily life.

Imagine mealtimes infused with gratitude, bedtime stories woven with biblical narratives, and even mundane chores transformed into lessons in service and cooperation. By integrating faith into the fabric of everyday life, parents become the architects of a home where faith isn't confined to a designated hour but blossoms continuously through shared moments and experiences.

However, this basic, homegrown approach does necessitate acknowledging its limitations. Single parents, struggling families, and individuals lacking strong family support systems may find navigating this framework challenging. Additionally, relying solely on family units as incubators for faith carries the risk of overlooking the essential role of the church community in providing support, mentorship, and a sense of belonging beyond the immediate family circle.

Therefore, family ministry must fully acknowledge its interconnectedness with the broader church community. While empowering families remains paramount, fostering open communication, offering resources and support beyond the family unit, and encouraging intergenerational interaction within the church become crucial in ensuring that no individual feels isolated in their faith journey.

Ultimately, the theology of family ministry recognizes the immense potential of the family as a fertile ground for nurturing faith. It empowers parents, celebrates diverse family structures, and encourages the integration of faith into daily life.

STRENGTHS AND WEAKNESSES

STRENGTHS

- Provides a focused approach to equipping parents as faith leaders.
- Emphasizes the importance of intentional faith formation within the family unit.

- Promotes intergenerational faith transmission and shared religious experiences.

WEAKNESSES

- May struggle to reach individuals lacking strong nuclear family support systems.
- Can be less adaptable to non-traditional family structures.
- Relies heavily on parents' commitment and engagement.

❖ PART 2: A THEOLOGY OF FAMILY CHURCH

Church as an Extended Family

Imagine stepping into a warm haven, not built from bricks and mortar, but woven from the threads of shared faith and unconditional love. This is the vision of the family church, where the walls of the sanctuary transform into the embrace of an extended family, welcoming individuals of all ages and backgrounds to find belonging and support beyond the boundaries of blood ties.

The echo of John 13:34-35 resonates within these walls: *"A new commandment I give you: Love one another. As I have loved you, so you must love one another. By this all will know that you are my disciples, if you have love for one another."* This verse becomes the guiding melody, its notes woven into every interaction, from shared laughter during potlucks to words of comfort in moments of need.

A Shared Spiritual Experience

Worship and learning take on a vibrant hue in this family setting. Services surprisingly bloom and blossom with intergenerational harmonies, where grandparents hum hymns alongside grandchildren, and teenagers engage in spirited theological debates during youth group. Sunday school transforms into a bustling marketplace of faith, where stories of Noah's ark come alive for little ones while adults delve deeper into scripture in dedicated studies. Mentors emerge from within the community, not just pastors, but seasoned members who offer guidance and encouragement like spiritual way finders, leading individuals on their unique journeys of faith.

J.I. Packer's words hold particular resonance here: *"Theology begins at home, and the family is the first seminary."* The family church expands upon this notion, suggesting that faith blossoms not just within biological units, but also within the broader community of the church family. Each individual, regardless of their family structure, becomes a thread woven into the vibrant fabric of a shared faith life.

Holistic and Adaptable Embrace

This embrace extends beyond doctrinal teachings, reaching into the practicalities of life. Crisis counseling and emergency assistance stand ready to catch those facing unexpected storms, their compassion a safety net woven from the collective strength of the community. Meals are shared, childcare offered, and burdens lifted, as church members become hands and feet of Jesus, demonstrating love through tangible acts of kindness.

Recognizing the diversity of families and cultural contexts, the family church thrives on adaptability. It embraces single parents, blended families, and non-traditional structures, tailoring its approach to meet the unique needs of each member. In this way, it bridges the gap between the ideal and the reality, ensuring that no one feels alone in their faith journey.

Key Characteristics of Family Church Theology

- **Family as a Vital Unit.** The family is not just a unit within the church, but a cornerstone. Its health and strength are seen as crucial to the overall well-being of the church community.

- **Worship and Learning as a Family.** Shared experiences strengthen the bonds of faith. Churches with this theology promote worship and learning activities that cater to all ages and encourage intergenerational participation.

- **Spiritual Influencers.** Parents, grandparents, and friends diverse individuals play crucial roles in connecting members to the broader community and guiding them closer to their faith.

- **A Supportive Church Community.** Church becomes an extension of the individual family. It which a safety net of support. It also encourages Church Members to find solace, understanding, and practical assistance in times of need.

- **Practical Application of Our Faith.** Faith isn't merely theoretical; it's woven into the fabric of everyday life. Family church theology emphasizes living out one's faith through acts of love, service, and ethical conduct.

- **Crisis and Counseling Support.** Recognizing the many vulnerabilities of families, this theology integrates pastoral care and counseling services into its framework, offering guidance and support during challenging times.

- **Holistic Approach.** Faith flourishes when nurtured in all aspects of life. Family church theology takes a holistic approach, addressing not just the individual's spiritual development but also their relational and communal well-being.
- **Valuing the Need for Celebration.** The celebration of birthdays, baptisms, graduations and other significant life events become occasions for community-wide celebration.
- **Rejoicing Together as a Family.** The church family rejoices together, strengthening the bonds of shared joy and support.
- **Adaptability.** Recognizing the diversity of families, family church theology adapts its approach to be inclusive and supportive of various structures and cultural contexts.

A Shared Love and Shared Grace

The family church theology paints a breathtaking picture of a community where love transcends bloodlines, where support stretches beyond immediate circles, and where faith finds fertile ground in the richness of shared experiences. It envisions a community where every individual, regardless of their family constellation, finds a place to call home, a haven where they can flourish and grow in the warmth of a shared spiritual family.

STRENGTHS AND WEAKNESSES

STRENGTHS

- Provides a strong support system for individuals lacking strong family ties.
- Offers a sense of belonging and community for diverse individuals.

- Fosters intergenerational connections and shared spiritual experiences.

Weaknesses

- May require stronger leadership and organizational structure to address individual needs.
- Balancing individual and group needs can be challenging.
- Maintaining long-term engagement of diverse members can be complex.

The Conclusion

Both family ministry and family church theologies play vital roles in fostering faith and community within the church realm. Each approach boasts unique strengths and weaknesses, making them suitable for different contexts and needs. Recognizing these distinctions and leveraging their respective strengths empowers churches to serve diverse families and individuals, effectively creating spaces where everyone feels nurtured, supported, and connected.

CHAPTER THREE

THE HISTORIC FABRIC AND BLUEPRINT
A Historical Foundation for the Family Church

Within the collage of faith that African Americans have assembled through centuries, the church holds a unique and enduring thread. More than just a denominational label or a Sunday morning gathering, it has been a sanctuary, a schoolhouse, a beacon of hope, and, most importantly, family. Tracing the historical relationship between African Americans and their local churches unveils a story of resilience, adaptation, and unwavering faith that forms the bedrock for understanding the contemporary concept of the family church.

Today, our traditional perceptions of the church face a crossroads. While vibrant contemporary expressions cater to shifting needs and preferences, they often overlook the historical core that defines the African American religious experience. At its heart, the church was not built on large-scale productions or transient membership. It thrived on small-group empowerment, fostering deep, long-lasting bonds within a community that felt like family. Ownership, commitment, and a sense of belonging resonated throughout these sacred spaces, offering a stark contrast to the increasingly fragmented landscape of modern society.

Yet, in this very fragmentation lies an opportunity. The yearning for connection, for community, for a deeper sense of belonging echoes the experiences of enslaved families ripped apart and forced to forge new bonds within the church walls. Back then, the church wasn't simply an extension of family; it became the family itself. Individuals, related or not, found solace, support, and identity within this community of faith. It nurtured not just their souls but also their social, economic, and educational needs.

Looking at the state of the modern African American family, with its rising single-parent households, divorce rates, and grandparent-led homes, a chilling parallel emerges. Though vastly different in context, the current situation shares unsettling similarities with the fractured landscapes of our early American experience. This is where the family church steps into the light, poised to reclaim and reimagine itself in a way that honors tradition while addressing contemporary needs.

The historical fabric of the African American church offers a blueprint for a renewed model. Here, the church re-establishes its role as an extended family, filling the gaps left by fractured social systems. It becomes a haven for education, social support, and economic guidance, stepping in where schools and government programs falter. Remember, for generations, the church was the stage for aspirations, the platform for learning new skills, the only place where one could truly feel valued and important. In a society where systemic barriers have historically marginalized African

Americans, the church offered a unique sanctuary, a safety net woven from the threads of shared faith and communal care.

This legacy isn't nostalgic romanticization; it's an authentic, living testament to the transformative power of faith and community. By drawing upon this historical wellspring, the family church can reclaim its central role in the lives of African Americans, offering much more than Sunday sermons and inspirational songs. The family church can become a haven where families, both traditional and unconventional, find refuge, support, and a sense of belonging in a world that often feels fragmented and isolating.

As we explore the intricacies of the family church within the African American context, this chapter delves into the rich mosaic of its history. We examine the unique challenges and triumphs faced by these communities, highlighting the crucial role the church played in fostering resilience and progress. Through historical accounts, personal narratives, and theological insights, we paint a vivid picture of this enduring connection, demonstrating how the past offers invaluable lessons for navigating the present and shaping a brighter future for the family church in the African American community.

This journey through the historical foundation of the family church isn't merely an academic exercise; it's a call to action. It invites us to rediscover the transformative power of community, to rekindle the flames of shared faith, and to construct a new paradigm of support and belonging for generations to come. So, let us step into the past, not with dusty nostalgia, but with open hearts and curious minds, ready to learn, reimagine, and reclaim the essence of the family church for the African American community of today and the generations to come.

To fully grasp the potential of the family church within the African American community, we must examine it through a multifaceted lens. Firstly, we look back at its historical roots, recognizing the larger context of faith and resilience interwoven into the fabric of African American experience. Here, the church wasn't simply a building; it was a sanctuary, a schoolhouse, a beacon of hope for communities navigating the tumultuous waters of slavery and segregation. In this historical lens, the family church emerges as a vital force, birthed from the need for connection, support, and identity in the face of systematic oppression.

Secondly, we focus on the specific lens of the African Methodist Episcopal Church (AME Church), a vibrant faith tradition that exemplifies the essence of the family church. Founded in 1816, the AME Church prioritized the empowerment of individuals and families, fostering a sense of ownership and belonging within its congregations. It served as a model for social engagement, advocating for education, economic justice, and political participation. In its heyday, the AME Church pulsated with the energy of a communal family, offering not just spiritual guidance but also practical support systems for its members. By examining the family church through these dual lenses — the broader historical experience and the specific example of the AME Church — we gain a deeper understanding of its potential for transformation. We see it as an institution deeply rooted in resilience, adapting to the needs of its community while holding fast to its core values of love, support, and shared faith.

As we turn the pages of this chapter, we embark on a journey through the rich history of the family church within the African American community. We explore the triumphs and challenges of the past, learning valuable lessons about building strong families and resilient communities. We delve into the specific contributions of the AME Church, celebrating its commitment to empowerment and social justice. Through these historical lenses, we discover how the family church can become more than just a Sunday morning gathering; it can be a transformative force, constructing a vibrant foundation of faith, support, and belonging for generations to come.

THE BLACK CHURCH: A BASTION OF FAITH AND FAMILY IN THE SHADOW OF SLAVERY

The mosaic of African American history is a tale of resilience, made stronger in the face of unimaginable hardship. Within this saga, the Black church shines as a beacon of unwavering faith, a sanctuary against the storms of slavery, and a crucible where shattered families were reforged. To understand the early experience of Black people in America, one must acknowledge the crucial role the church played in sustaining families, nurturing cultural identity, and igniting the embers of resistance.

Shattered Bonds and the Balm of Faith

The institution of slavery sought to extinguish the very essence of family. Separations ripped parents from children, siblings from one another, leaving wounds that bled in the silence of sun-drenched fields. Yet, within the walls of the Black church, a glimmer of family flickered back to life. Here, amidst shared hymns and whispered prayers, fragmented families found solace and rekindled a sense of belonging. Sunday sermons became pronouncements of kinship, echoing the words of John 13:34-35, *"Love one another. As I have loved you, so you must love one another."* This love manifested in shared burdens, whispered joys, and a collective identity that transcended individual circumstance.

Candles in the Darkness: Nurturing Rites and Traditions

Ceremonies, once the cornerstones of family life, were brutally disrupted by the whims of slave owners. Births, marriages, and deaths were often mourned or celebrated in stolen moments, away from prying eyes. But the Black church offered a safe haven for these sacred rituals. Baptismal fonts witnessed the entry of new life into the community, echoing the promise of a future beyond the shackles of bondage. Weddings, though stripped of pomp and extravagance, affirmed the sanctity of love and family, defying the dehumanizing gaze of oppression. Funerals, steeped in the sorrow of loss, became testaments to the enduring spirit of a community, ensuring that loved ones were not simply forgotten but sent on their final journey surrounded by the warmth of a shared faith.

Hidden Fires of Education and Empowerment

Literacy, a gateway to knowledge and power, was weaponized by slave owners, who feared the potential of empowered minds. Yet, within the shadows of the church, clandestine murmurs of letters and numbers exchanged hands. Ministers, risking punishment and persecution, lit the embers of education, teaching enslaved individuals to read and write. This stolen knowledge became a tool of resistance, a passport to a broader understanding of the world, and a beacon of hope for a future liberated from the chains of **injustice.**

A Landscape of Support: Strength in Shared Burdens

The burdens of slavery, heavy and oppressive, weighed upon families, threatening to crush their spirits. Yet, within the embrace of the Black church, a network of support emerged, woven from the threads of shared adversity. Mutual aid societies flourished, offering practical assistance with food, clothing, and healthcare. Elders, repositories of wisdom and resilience, mentored younger generations, passing down ancestral knowledge and stories of defiance. Through collective action and shared burdens, the church empowered families to endure, fostering a spirit of unity and a belief in their collective strength.

Finding Solace and Strength in the Divine

Slavery tore not only at the fabric of families but also at the human spirit. The fear, the loneliness, the constant threat of violence, and the gnawing despair could easily extinguish the fire of faith. Yet, within the church walls, individuals found solace in the embrace of a higher power. Ministers, often former slaves themselves, preached messages of hope and liberation, drawing upon biblical stories of oppression and deliverance. Spirituals, born from the depths of suffering, became anthems of resilience, their melodies carrying hopes of a promised land where shackles would be broken and chains would fall away.

Voices From the Pulpit and the Pew

The stories of resilience and faith echoed not only in the hushed voices of prayer but also in the pronouncements of iconic figures who found their voices within the church. Harriet Jacobs, in her searing narrative, spoke of the church as a refuge, a space where enslaved women found comfort and shared their burdens. Frederick Douglass, his voice booming from the pulpit, testified to the church's role in fostering community and igniting the embers of resistance. Sojourner Truth, her words as sharp as blades, spoke of the church as a training ground for activism, nurturing her strength and resolve in the fight for freedom and equality.

Nat Turner, driven by both faith and outrage, envisioned the church as a wellspring of righteous anger, leading a rebellion fueled by the yearning for liberation. Elizabeth Keckley, her voice tinged with bittersweet memories, described the church as a source of solace and hope for enslaved individuals, a space where camaraderie and shared faith offered a flicker of light in the darkness. Henry "Box" Brown, his journey to freedom testament to the human spirit's tenacity, acknowledged the church.

THE BEACON IN THE STORM: THE AFRICAN METHODIST EPISCOPAL CHURCH AND THE FAMILY CHURCH IDEAL

From the ashes of oppression and the yearning for freedom, the African Methodist Episcopal (AME) Church rose as a beacon, not just for spiritual solace but for a collective African American identity and a vital force in the family church ideal. Founded in 1787 by Richard Allen and Absalom Jones, the AME Church became more than a place of worship; it was a crucible where resilience was forged, communities thrived, and generations of leaders emerged, forever shaping the landscape of Black America.

❖ Richard Allen: Pioneering a Legacy of Empowerment

Richard Allen, a former slave and the AME Church's first bishop, laid the foundation for its family church mission. Recognizing the fragmented families wrought by slavery, Allen established ministries that catered to their well-being. Educational initiatives nurtured intellectual growth and empowered individuals. Social justice activism, fueled by Allen's own fight for freedom, tackled racial inequality and injustice, creating a space for collective action and social progress. Community support ministries provided practical assistance, from food distribution to financial aid, alleviating the burdens faced by families struggling under societal pressures. Spiritual formation and discipleship programs fostered strong, faith-based individuals, building a core of resilience within the congregation. And recognizing the importance of nurturing the next generation, Allen initiated youth and family ministries, strengthening familial bonds and fostering a supportive community for children.

❖ **From Tragedy to Triumph: Rebuilding Lives, Families, and Communities**

In 1916, the Tulsa Race Massacre devastated the Greenwood District, a thriving Black community in Oklahoma. In the aftermath, the AME Church played a pivotal role in rebuilding both physical structures and shattered spirits. Churches served as temporary shelters and kitchens, offering safe haven and sustenance to the displaced. Ministers provided counseling and spiritual guidance, helping individuals cope with the trauma and find the strength to rebuild. This response embodied the family church ideal at its core, demonstrating its capacity to bind up wounds, restore hope, and lead communities from tragedy to a new dawn.

❖ **A Chorus of Leaders: Guiding the Flock and Lighting the Way**

Throughout its history, the AME Church has been blessed with visionary leaders who embodied the family church ideal in their journeys and contributions. Bishop Daniel Alexander Payne, a notable educator, played a pivotal role in establishing Wilberforce University, empowering the minds of generations of Black youth. Bishop Vashti Murphy McKenzie, the first woman bishop in the AME Church, shattered glass ceilings while advocating for social justice, women's empowerment, and community engagement, her leadership transforming the church's communication and outreach in the face of modern challenges. Bishop Henry McNeal Turner, a fervent advocate for Black nationalism and self-determination, actively participated in political and civil rights causes, mobilizing the community towards social progress. Bishop Sarah Frances Davis, a pioneer in education and civil rights, paved the way for women in church leadership while tirelessly serving her community. This amalgam of visionary leaders, diverse in their contributions yet united in their commitment to uplifting the Black community, exemplifies the very essence of the family church ideal.

❖ From Pulpit to Community: Seeds of Inspiration

The impact of the AME Church transcended its walls, inspiring individuals who carried its teachings and dedication into the wider community. Cecil "Chip" Murray, pastor of the First African Methodist Episcopal (FAME) Church in Los Angeles, transformed his congregation into a hub for development, economic empowerment, and social justice. His initiatives tackled education, healthcare, and economic inequality, leaving an indelible mark on the lives of Black Angelenos. A. Philip Randolph, a preacher's son and prominent figure in the civil rights and labor movements, exemplified the commitment to social justice ingrained in the AME Church tradition. His leadership in organizing the March on Washington and advocating for workers' rights resonated with the church's call for collective action and empowerment. From renowned academics like Benjamin Banneker and Benjamin Tucker Tanner to trailblazing entrepreneurs like Bridget "Biddy" Mason and community icons like Daisy Lee Gaston Bates, the AME Church fostered a spirit of service and leadership that touched every facet of Black life.

❖ Cultivating Hope: Transforming Families

Bishop T. Larry Kirkland provides a powerful example of the transformative power of the "family church" model within the AME Church. In 1977, he was appointed pastor of Brookins Community AME Church in Los Angeles. At the time, the congregation consisted of a mere eight members, borrowed from another church. However, under Bishop Kirkland's leadership, the church experienced phenomenal growth. By the time he was elected Bishop in 1996, the congregation had blossomed to over 8,000 members.

What was the secret to this remarkable transformation? Bishop Kirkland himself attributes it not to personal charisma, but to the power of God and the intentional cultivation of a strong "family church" environment. This emphasis on creating a family atmosphere was nurtured through the establishment of various ministries that catered to all ages and needs.

Early on, he focused on foundational ministries like Sunday School, the Women's Missionary Society, and a Youth Department. These groups provided opportunities for spiritual growth, fellowship, and service within a supportive community. Recognizing the importance of ongoing engagement, Bishop Kirkland also established the New Members Institute and Welcome Club, facilitating integration and connection for newcomers. Additionally, the Couples Club fostered strong marriages, while various outreach ministries extended the church's love and support beyond its walls.

❖ A Legacy of Togetherness: The Family Church Ideal in Full Bloom

The African American church, exemplified by the AME Church, stands as a testament to the transformative power of the family church ideal. It offered solace and belonging in the face of unimaginable hardship, nurtured cultural identity and resilience, and ignited the flames of resistance against oppression. From educational initiatives to social justice activism, from community support to spiritual guidance, the family church fostered a holistic sense of well-being that extended beyond the pews.

The stories of Bishop Richard Allen, Bishop Vashti Murphy McKenzie, and Chip Murray, interwoven with the achievements of countless others, paint a vibrant image of empowerment. They exemplify the power of faith, community, and collective action in overcoming adversity and forging a brighter future. Through its commitment to education, social justice, and spiritual growth, the African American church, particularly the AME Church, has not only nurtured strong families but also empowered generations to break barriers, rewrite narratives, and shape a world where equality and justice ring true.

The journey of the family church, woven from threads of hardship and hope, stands as a beacon of resilience and a testament to the enduring power of community. In the shadow of slavery, the church became a sanctuary, a schoolhouse, a soapbox, and a sanctuary. Its leaders, from pulpit to community, ignited the flames of empowerment, and its members, nurtured by faith and fueled by a collective spirit, rose to become changemakers and advocates for the community.

❖ Beyond Walls: Global Reach and Enduring Impact

The influence of the AME Church extends far beyond the borders of the United States. It has established congregations around the world, fostering faith, education, and social justice initiatives in diverse communities. From Liberia to South Africa, AME missionaries and leaders have helped empower local communities, fight against oppression, and advocate for human rights. This global reach underscores the universal appeal of the family church model, showcasing its ability to transcend cultural and geographical boundaries to offer solace, connection, and empowerment wherever it takes root.

These are just a few glimpses into the vast chronicle of the family church ideal as embodied by the AME Church. From fostering individual journeys of triumph to driving collective transformation within communities, its impact resonates in countless lives across generations. In a world that often seeks to divide, the family church stands as a powerful testament to the strength found in unity, the transformative power of faith, and the enduring legacy of those who dared to dream of a better future.

"Imagine embarking on a pilgrimage, not to a physical destination, but towards a community where hearts meet, spirits intertwine, and faith blossoms in the fertile ground of shared experience."

CHAPTER FOUR

BUILDING A FAMILY CHURCH - TEN INSIGHTS
A Journey of Connection and Growth

Imagine embarking on a pilgrimage, not to a physical destination, but towards a community where hearts meet, spirits intertwine, and faith blossoms in the fertile ground of shared experience. This is the journey of building a family church, a sanctuary where Sunday sermons are merely seeds sown during weekly gatherings that extend far beyond the pews. It's a path I've walked for twenty years, not with a map meticulously drawn, but with the lessons learned from each stumble and the joy gleaned from every triumph.

The edifice itself - the large frescoes and murals - may be impressive, but it's the unseen foundations, the invisible mortar of connection, that truly define a family church. This chapter lays bare ten essential insights, gleaned from countless interactions, late-night conversations, and moments of shared grief and celebration. These are not rigid decrees, but rather compass points for your own pilgrimage, guiding you towards a haven where love overflows from Sunday mornings and permeates the very fabric of everyday life.

This is not a journey for the faint of heart. The path can be arduous, fraught with unexpected detours and occasional forks in the road. But the rewards are worth every step. Building a family church is about creating a space where individuals come not just to worship, but to belong. It's about fostering a community where burdens are shared, joys multiplied, and a sense of belonging takes root deeper than the pews can hold.

There's no cookie-cutter approach to navigating this terrain. Each church, like each family, is unique, shaped by its own history, traditions, and the diverse backgrounds of its members. Yet, certain guiding principles emerge from the depths of experience, becoming lighthouses in the fog of uncertainty. These are the insights I offer, not as blueprints to be rigidly followed, but as lanterns illuminating the path ahead.

First and foremost, remember that the heart of a family church beats not in its architecture, but in the depth of its relationships. It's in the lingering conversations over steaming cups of coffee after the service, in the helping hand extended during times of crisis, in the shared laughter at a potluck dinner. Cultivate an atmosphere where connection isn't merely encouraged, but actively nurtured. Let your church be a space where strangers become friends, friends become family, and family becomes the bedrock upon which faith thrives.

Next, remember that harmony is the lifeblood of any community. Discord, like a creeping frost, can wither the most vibrant fellowship. Prioritize a sanctuary of peace, not just within the walls of your church, but also in the interactions between members. Let every encounter, from the usher greeting newcomers to the kitchen volunteers sharing smiles, be infused with respect, affirmation, and genuine concern. Remember, your church is a sacred space, a haven where all members deserve to feel safe and valued, children of God embraced by a loving community.

These are just the first steps on the path, mere glimpses into the ten insights that have illuminated my own journey. As you delve deeper into this book, you will encounter lessons on the importance of vibrant youth ministries, the power of reaching out to missing faces, and the joy of forging bonds through shared celebrations. You will learn how to prioritize your resources to nourish the things that truly matter and the courage to experiment, venturing beyond the familiar to embrace opportunities for growth.

Ultimately, building a family church is not about reaching a preordained destination, but about cultivating a continuous journey of connection and growth. It's about creating a space where faith finds fertile ground in the shared soil of everyday life, where love transcends Sunday mornings and blossoms in a symphony of human experience. So, take heart, fellow traveler, and embark on this pilgrimage with me. Let these insights be your guideposts, your compass as you navigate the sometimes treacherous but ultimately rewarding path towards building a church that becomes not just a place of worship, but a family, a home, a beacon of love in the world.

This journey awaits, full of laughter, tears, shared meals, and whispered prayers. Join me, and together, let's build a family church where every member feels not just counted, but truly counted on, where lives intertwine, and faith flourishes under the warm, unwavering light of shared love.

INSIGHT NUMBER ONE

PUT THE PEOPLE FIRST - SHARING THE PATH TOGETHER

A family church isn't just a destination; it's a shared journey, a winding path where individuals become fellow travelers, their lives and stories intertwining under the expansive sky of faith. Unlike churches that feel like fleeting rest stops on a busy highway, where Sunday sermons are quick refuels before returning to the race, family churches offer a welcoming sanctuary, a place where you're invited to linger, to plant your roots, and embark on a collective pilgrimage deeper into the heart of community.

Here, life's milestones aren't mere mile markers on a solitary trek; they're shared peaks ascended together; valleys navigated with a chorus of encouragement. Graduation gowns billow not just for the individual but for the community that cheered them on each step of the climb. Retirement parties become celebratory pit stops, moments to pause and reflect on the shared journey, a landscape rich with the memories of friends and loved ones. Births and weddings aren't solo expeditions; they're joyous departures on new paths, with the entire community gathered to shower blessings and offer maps for the uncharted territory ahead. And in moments of darkness, when grief clouds the path, the community becomes a sturdy lantern, illuminating the way, offering a steady hand to guide through the treacherous terrain.

Building this kind of journey-based church isn't about boasting the stained-glass windows or offering the most polished itinerary. It's about putting the people first, recognizing that the true heart of the pilgrimage lies not in the grandeur of the destination, but in the richness of the connections forged along the way. It's about valuing the diverse talents, experiences, and stories carried by each traveler, for it is these collective treasures that illuminate the path and nurture the spirit of fellowship.

Think of our members not as mere passengers on a pre-packaged tour, but as fellow explorers, each holding a unique compass, each equipped with skills and strengths that can enrich the journey for all. They are the storytellers who share their personal narratives around crackling campfires, the cartographers who map uncharted paths of service, the navigators who steer the community through moments of doubt and uncertainty. By recognizing and empowering these vibrant talents, we transform our church from a passive sightseeing bus into a dynamic expedition, where every member has a role to play in shaping the shared adventure.

But such a journey doesn't unfold magically. It requires intentionality, a deliberate focus on creating opportunities for shared experiences, moments where individual paths converge and hearts connect. It means building campfire circles of small group gatherings, where vulnerabilities are shared and journeys compared, forging bonds deeper than casual exchanges. It means setting up trailheads of service projects, where talents find expression and lives are transformed through acts of collective good will. Each of these shared experiences, like sturdy ropes thrown across canyons of division, bind us closer, strengthening the fabric of our pilgrim community.

Putting people first, then, isn't just a feel-good sentiment; it's the very compass point that guides our collective trek. It ensures that birthdays and anniversaries become not just calendar entries, but cherished stops on the shared path, celebrated with laughter and song. It means that weddings aren't simply isolated ceremonies, but departures witnessed by a loving chorus, their echoes reverberating through the valleys of our shared journey. And when grief casts its shadow, it's not met with solitary despair; the ropes of connection hold firm, offering a sturdy hand and a chorus of murmured prayers to lighten the load.

Ultimately, putting people first isn't a destination; it's the constant, unwavering commitment to making the journey itself one of connection, support, and shared growth. It's about recognizing that our fellow travelers are not just faces in the crowd, but companions on the path, their stories intricately woven into a shared pilgrimage. Only then can we truly claim to have built a family church, not a gilded sanctuary, but a vibrant community where lives unfold together, where faith illuminates the path, and where love becomes the guiding star that leads us all, hand in hand, towards the sun-dappled horizon of hope.

PROTECT THE ATMOSPHERE - A HAVEN OF HARMONY AND HOPE

Imagine a sanctuary, not carved from stone and stained glass, but woven from the delicate threads of peace and harmony. A refuge from the world's cacophony, where weary souls, burdened by life's trials, find solace in the resonant silence of shared love and respect. This is the atmosphere we must strive for in a family church, a sacred space where friction finds no purchase, and discord is chased away by the gentle breeze of understanding and kindness.

For a church's true strength lies not in its imposing architecture or polished programs, but in the tangible peace it offers. It's a haven where the weary traveler, carrying the baggage of career stresses, marital strains, and unfulfilled dreams, lays them down at the entrance, greeted not by a frosty air of tension, but by the warmth of acceptance and mutual regard.

A sanctuary choked with tension and friction becomes a breeding ground for disunity and stagnation. Imagine stepping into this space for the first time, not seeking the comforting embrace of faith, but encountering icy stares of discord. The sermon may preach love, the choir may *sing of hope*, but the palpable tension can whisper doubts about the authenticity of such pronouncements. The seeking heart yearns for a refuge, not a battlefield of unspoken disagreements.

This is why protecting the atmosphere of our family church becomes paramount. It's not about stifling healthy debate or enforcing a superficial harmony. It's about prioritizing respect, affirmational interactions, and genuine concern, not just within our inner circle, but throughout the mosaic of our community.

From the bustling hum of the kitchen ministry to the quiet efficiency of the parking lot attendants, from the welcoming smiles of the ushers to the compassionate words of the stewards, every interaction within our church should be infused with respect and dignity. Remember, while everyone won't become your closest confidante, each person who enters this sacred space deserves to be treated with the worth inherent in every child of God.

This isn't just about upholding etiquette; it's about creating a tangible testament to the transformative power of faith. Imagine the impact on a visitor entering our doors, not greeted by icy stares and hushed gossip, but by a chorus of warm hellos and genuine interest. Imagine the skeptic, hardened by past disappointments, witnessing not a battlefield of petty squabbles, but a community bound by love and support, where differences are acknowledged with grace and unity prevails over discord.

This is the atmosphere we must cultivate, not through draconian rules or forced smiles, but through a conscious commitment to kindness, understanding, and active listening. It's about fostering open communication, where grievances are addressed with respect and disagreements are navigated with compassion. It's about remembering that within every member lies a story, a journey worthy of understanding and a heart yearning for connection.

Protecting this atmosphere isn't a luxury; it's a necessity. It's the fertile ground where faith flourishes, where hearts open to vulnerability, and where forgiveness takes root. It's the gentle breeze that blows away the seeds of doubt and nourishes the fruits of love and hope.

So, let us walk through the doors of our church not just as members or leaders, but as guardians of this precious atmosphere. Let us be the weavers of harmony, the builders of bridges, and the cultivators of genuine care. Let us strive not just for polished sermons and impressive outreach programs, but for a sanctuary where the tangible peace exemplifies a deeper truth, a testament to the transformative power of love and the unwavering presence of God.

INSIGHT NUMBER THREE

YOUTH MINISTRIES MATTER - CULTIVATING SEEDS OF FAITH

Imagine a journey, not through miles and continents, but through the uncharted terrain of childhood and adolescence. A time of stumbling steps, blossoming dreams, and hearts ripe with the potential for both beauty and rebellion. This is the path our young travelers walk, and within the landscape of a family church, we have the privilege of being their companions, their guides, and their unwavering advocates. For within the vibrant confines of a thriving youth ministry lies the very promise of our church's future.

In an era where demographics shift and traditions seem to fade, a strong and engaging youth ministry becomes not just a desirable attribute, but a vital lifeblood for a family church. This isn't simply about numbers, though the dwindling presence of younger generations cannot be ignored. It's about recognizing the unique gifts and energies that young people bring to our community, their vitality a breath of fresh air, their perspectives a lens unclouded by cynicism, and their enthusiasm a spark that can ignite the embers of faith in all generations.

Think of our church as an incubator, a nurturing haven where seeds of faith are not just sown, but cultivated with loving care. It's a space where talents find expression, be it through the joy of music, the laughter of fellowship, or the quiet contemplation of scripture. It's a platform where leadership skills blossom, where young voices rise in confident debates and find their place in shaping the future of our community.

But the benefits are not one-sided. Just as the church offers a sanctuary for youthful exploration, our young travelers become ambassadors of faith, weaving the threads of love and joy back into the fabric of their homes. Often, before parents or grandparents find their way to the pews, it's a child's enthusiasm, their excited stories of games and lessons, that sparks curiosity and opens hearts to the possibility of fellowship. They become evangelists not through polished sermons or theological treatises, but through the infectious joy of belonging, the genuine warmth of their newfound friendships, and the quiet strength of their growing faith.

This isn't to say that creating a vibrant youth ministry is a simple endeavor. It requires dedication, imagination, and a willingness to step outside the comfort zone of traditional programming. It means recognizing that the needs of today's youth are diverse and ever-evolving, demanding programs that engage their minds, bodies, and spirits. It means creating a space where questions are not met with judgement, but with open ears and compassionate hearts, where vulnerability is embraced and doubt is seen as a seedling of deeper faith.

Ultimately, investing in our youth ministry is not just about securing the future of the church; it's about fulfilling a sacred responsibility. It's about recognizing that every child entrusted to our care holds within them the potential for greatness, a spark of the divine waiting to be kindled. It's about providing the fertile ground, the nurturing light, and the gentle guidance that allows those seeds of faith to blossom into the flowers of tomorrow.

So, let us open our hearts and our doors to our young travelers, welcoming them not just as future leaders or potential recruits, but as treasured companions on this shared journey of faith. Let us be the builders of bridges, the weavers of laughter, and the cultivators of curiosity. Let us remember that their joy is our joy, their struggles our own, and their faith a reflection of the eternal hope that binds us all. For in nurturing our youth ministry, we not only secure the future of our church, but also develop within them the vibrant faith that will resonate through generations to come.

DON'T FORGET MISSING FACES - WEAVING STRENGTH FROM BROKEN THREADS

Imagine two travelers traversing a rugged terrain, their laughter echoing through the valleys as they share stories and dreams. But the path, while breathtaking, is fraught with challenges. One stumbles, twisting an ankle, pain etching lines on their face. Fear creeps in, a gnawing doubt about their ability to continue. In this moment, what defines the true essence of companionship? Do you abandon them to their struggle, the echoes of their cries fading into the wilderness? Or do you reach out, a hand extended in support, a shared burden easing the weight of the journey?

This is the heart of a family church. It's not just a haven for the strong and vibrant, but a sanctuary for the weary and wounded. It's a community where missing faces aren't simply empty pews, but threads unraveling from the fabric of our shared journey. They are the travelers who have stumbled, those whose burdens threaten to overwhelm them, those who yearn for a hand to grasp and a voice to whisper, *"you are not alone."*

For within a family church, love isn't just a *"sermoned"* ideal, but a tangible lifeline woven into the fabric of our relationships. It's the phone call placed to the silent number, the card tucked into a mailbox, the doorstep adorned with a bouquet of vibrant blooms. It's the gentle knock on a shut-in's door, the steaming plate of food delivered with a warm smile, the patient hand guiding them through the intricacies of a tablet, connecting them to the pulse of the community even from afar.

These gestures, born not from duty, but from genuine care, speak volumes. They whisper a simple truth: *"You are missed. You are remembered. You are part of us."* And in that quiet affirmation lies the power to mend hearts and rekindle hope.

Think of the missing faces not as burdens, but as threads calling out for repair. They are the stories hidden between lines of missed Sundays; the struggles buried beneath a facade of resilience. By reaching out, we pull these members back into the fold, strengthening the very fabric of our community.

For in their experiences, we find not just lessons in empathy, but testaments to the transformative power of love. They become witnesses to the world, sharing tales of a church where no soul is lost in the shadows, where burdens are shared, and where hope blooms even in the most barren moments. They become living proofs that love isn't confined to the pews, but spills out into the streets, a beacon of compassion in a world often shrouded in isolation.

So, let us open our hearts to the calamity of missing faces. Let us be weavers of connection, mending broken threads with acts of kindness and unwavering support. Let us remember that every empty pew represents a story, a journey interrupted, a heart yearning for a sense of belonging.

For in this act of remembrance and unwavering commitment to inclusivity, we build a sanctuary where no traveler, no matter how weary or wounded, is ever truly left behind.

INSIGHT NUMBER FIVE

FELLOWSHIP FEEDS THE SOUL - SHARING THE JOURNEY

Imagine two weary travelers, their paths intersecting not just for a fleeting moment on a busy train platform, but for the entire journey. They could choose to remain strangers, eyes cast down, lost in their own thoughts. But in the family church, this isn't the chosen path. Here, travelers choose to engage, opening their hearts and sharing their journey.

The family church becomes a haven for human connection, where the sterile air of anonymity is replaced by the warmth of shared laughter and whispered stories. It's not just about scheduled events or organized activities, though these moments provide fertile ground for fellowship. It's the small, spontaneous interactions that truly weave the threads of community.

The casual conversation by the coffee machine, the lingering lunch break spent sharing experiences, the impromptu prayer circle formed in response to a whispered need – these are the moments where strangers morph into companions, where faces etched in fleeting greetings become etched in shared vulnerability and joy.

This desire to truly know one another, to go beyond the surface pleasantries and delve into the depths of each other's stories, is what sets the family church apart. It's a space where birthdays spark impromptu celebrations, where graduation parties become communal triumphs, and where weddings weave new families into the existing community.

Imagine the strength built through these shared experiences, the invisible bonds forged in laughter and tears, in triumphs and tragedies. When a traveler stumbles, the community gathers, offering not just a helping hand, but a chorus of unwavering support. When joy blooms, it's not a solitary sunbeam, but a collective fireworks display, illuminating the shared path they tread.

This isn't about forced interactions or quickly orchestrated friendships. It's about creating a space where genuine connection can take root organic growth. It's about fostering a culture of care, where invitations are not obligations, but heartfelt desires to share the experiences of our lives.

The family church, then, transcends its physical walls to become a family in the truest sense. Here, differences fade in the shared light of love, where vulnerability isn't a weakness, but a bridge to deeper connection. Every traveler, no matter how seasoned or new to the journey, finds their place in the shared narrative, their voice welcomed, their story cherished.

So, let us be travelers who choose to engage, who extend not just a polite nod, but an open heart. Let us be the spark that ignites shared laughter, the patient ear that listens to whispered tales, and the steady hand that offers support in times of need.

For in nurturing this sacred space of fellowship, we build not just a church, but a family, a vibrant community where every soul finds not just a destination, but a shared journey filled with laughter, tears, and the unwavering comfort of knowing they are never truly alone.

INSIGHT NUMBER SIX

Money Follows Mission - Investing in Connection and Care

Imagine a seasoned camper packing their backpack for a long trek. Every item chosen earns its place – a tent for shelter, a map for guidance, food for sustenance. Each omission speaks volumes, revealing what isn't deemed essential for the journey.

The family church budget plays a similar role. It's not just a spreadsheet; it's a tangible reflection of our priorities, a declaration of what we value on this shared pilgrimage of faith. It's a compass, guiding us towards our mission of building a haven of connection and care.

Too often, church budgets prioritize appearances over essence. Lavish decorations, gourmet meals, glitter, and flashy entertainment overshadow the true soul of a family church – fellowship, inclusion, and genuine care for all members, regardless of age or financial contribution.

These aren't mere luxuries; they're the cornerstone of building a family. While quality food and engaging activities have their place, the heart of a thriving community lies in the spontaneous laughter shared over a humble potluck, the meaningful conversations that blossom around a simple cup of coffee, the genuine connection forged in shared laughter and tears.

Yes, the budget must cover operational costs and essential needs. But the family church understands that extravagant displays don't equate to spiritual growth. Instead, it prioritizes strategic and efficient resource allocation, investing in initiatives that foster connection, support vulnerable groups like children and seniors, and nurture a welcoming atmosphere for all.

Imagine the potential of a budget that prioritizes youth programs, creating avenues for spiritual exploration and fostering a sense of belonging. Picture a budget that allocates resources to outreach initiatives, welcoming newcomers with open arms and bridging the gap between isolation and community. Consider a budget that invests in care programs for seniors, ensuring their needs are met and their voices heard.

These investments aren't mere expenses; they're seeds sown in fertile ground. They promise strong roots, reaching out to connect individuals and nurturing the delicate blossoms of faith in all generations. It's not about extravagance, but about intentionality, about ensuring every dollar translates into genuine connection and tangible care for all members of our spiritual family.

The family church budget isn't just a list of figures; it's a narrative, a story of our deepest values unfolding on a page. It's a roadmap to a future where we stand not as a collection of individuals, but as a community of shared laughter, unwavering support, and unwavering care. It's a statement that declares: *"Here, connection and fellowship aren't luxuries — they're the cornerstones of our shared journey."*

So, let us examine our budget not just through financial lenses, but through the lens of our mission. Let us allocate resources with intentionality, prioritizing investments that build bridges, nurture bonds, and ensure that every member, regardless of age or background, feels cherished and cared for within the family.

By placing our financial support where our mission dictates, we don't just write numbers on a page; we write a beautiful chapter in the ongoing story of a community bound by love, support, and unwavering faith.

POWER IN FOCUS - LESS IS MORE FOR MAXIMUM IMPACT

Imagine our family church as a bustling tour bus, eager to take its diverse passengers on a journey of faith and fellowship. Initially, the driver prioritizes individual preferences, scheduling tours based on each group's desired landmarks and stops. However, a disheartening sight emerges: *the bus, designed for vibrant encounters, is perpetually half-empty, echoing with the hollow sound of missed connections.*

This scattered approach, while well-intentioned, dilutes the experience for everyone. The driver, recognizing the magic that unfolds in a full bus, decides on a shift in strategy. He opts for *"addition by subtraction,"* a bold move that prioritizes quality over quantity.

Instead of catering to individual schedules, he creates carefully curated itineraries, consolidating offerings and scheduling key events on shared days. Sunday mornings become bustling hubs, with Sunday school seamlessly woven into the fabric of worship, followed by a potluck where connections bloom over steaming dishes. Special days shed their isolated afternoons, finding vibrant new life within the morning service, their message reaching the entire congregation instead of a dwindling few.

The benefits are immediate. The once-lonely bus explodes with life, laughter weaving through conversations, shared experiences strengthening the bonds of community. Fewer trips minimize costs, while human resources, precious and limited, are now concentrated, creating a synergy that elevates each program.

But *"addition by subtraction"* isn't about mere reduction. It's about strategic focusing. By consolidating, we don't eliminate; we amplify. Each ministry becomes a magnet, drawing its network and families into the shared space, boosting attendance and support for all. Imagine the choir performing not to empty pews, but to a captivated congregation, their music resonating with newfound power. Picture the youth ministry, no longer isolated, finding enthusiastic mentors and a supportive audience among fellow church members.

Our busy, fragmented lives might tempt us to cling to scattered schedules and dispersed offerings. Yet, it's the concentrated moments, the shared spaces, which hold the true alchemy of community. By subtracting redundant trips, we add vibrant connections. By eliminating what dilutes our impact, we magnify the message that binds us.

This *"addition by subtraction"* isn't a retreat, but a rediscovery of our core strength. It's a return to the essence of the family church, where diverse journeys converge, where laughter echoes through shared hallways, and where connections forged in focus ignite a faith that resounds far beyond the walls of our church.

INSIGHT NUMBER EIGHT

LEARNING ON THE TRAIL - NAVIGATING THE PATHS OF INNOVATION

Imagine a band of travelers standing at the crossroads of Mini Fork Road. Trails snake out before them, each promising adventures unseen. The path behind, familiar but stagnant, beckons with the comfort of the known. Yet, a choice must be made – to stand still, forever tethered to the familiar, or to venture onto the untrodden paths, embracing the potential and perils of the unknown.

The family church faces a similar quandary. Building a vibrant community in an ever-evolving landscape demands more than merely repeating past successes. It necessitates an adventurous spirit, a willingness to embrace the words of Samuel Beckett: *"Ever tried. Ever failed. No matter. Try again. Fail again. Fail better."*

For within the heart of every failed program lies a lesson waiting to be learned. Every misstep marks a path not to be blindly followed again, but a detour offering valuable insights on the journey towards building a true family church.

This isn't an encouragement to reckless experimentation. Rather, it's a call for calculated risk-taking, informed by careful planning and rigorous analysis. Pilot new programs, observe their impact, analyze their strengths and weaknesses. Discard what doesn't resonate, refine what shows promise, and iterate relentlessly in pursuit of excellence.

Family churches cannot afford the luxury of paralysis. To stand still is to wither, to shrink in the face of a world brimming with evolving needs and aspirations. Each community is a unique ecosystem, demanding tailored ministries and initiatives. What thrives in one church might falter in another. Only through experimentation, through venturing down unexplored paths, can we discover the ministry mix that truly resonates with our community.

This important journey takes time. Family churches don't sprout overnight; they blossom one seed at a time, one shared meal, one joyful song, one heartfelt conversation. Cultivating these seeds requires patience, a commitment to nurture each program, allowing it to mature and reach its full potential.

Investing in ongoing development isn't a drain on resources; it's a strategic application of them. By equipping volunteers and empowering lay leaders, we build a community of capable hands, freeing up pastors and staff to engage with members and shepherd their spiritual growth.

This isn't a call for reckless abandon, but for calculated exploration. Learning through trial and error isn't failure; it's the fuel that propels us forward. Every misstep, every wrong turn, becomes a beacon for future travelers, illuminating the path ahead.

So, let us embrace the spirit of the intrepid traveler, equipped with courage, curiosity, and a thirst for knowledge. Let us not shy away from the uncharted paths, for within them lie the seeds of innovation, the potential to build a vibrant family church that thrives in the ever-changing landscape of faith.

By venturing beyond the familiar, by learning from every step, by failing better with each turn, we pave the way for a future where every member finds their place, their voice amplified, and their faith nurtured within the welcoming embrace of our family church.

BEYOND THE PEW - EMBRACING THE CALL TO SHARE

Imagine an avid hiker, meticulously outfitted for adventure. She boasts top-tier gear, has mastered survival skills, and devoured every hiking manual under the sun. Yet, year after year, her meticulously packed backpack sits untouched, her hiking boots gather dust. The thrill of the trail remains a promise unfulfilled, her passion trapped in the realm of preparation.

Our churches sometimes resemble this hesitant hiker. We meticulously craft programs, invest in resources, and diligently train our members. Choirs rehearse hymns, Bible studies delve into scripture, and fellowship thrives within welcoming walls. Yet, when it comes to inviting others to share this experience of faith, a curious hesitation takes hold.

The Great Commission is our clarion call: *"Go therefore and make disciples of all nations."* But if our vibrant community remains confined within the familiar pews, if the light of Christ shines solely on our existing congregation, are we not like the hiker, forever poised on the brink of the journey but never taking the first step?

Growing, thriving churches understand that outreach and evangelism are not mere add-ons; they are the beating heart of our mission. To be a family church is to recognize that our faith isn't meant to be hoarded, but shared. It's like a fire, meant to spread warmth and illumination beyond its source.

Acknowledging this reality isn't a defeat, but a potent starting point. We must shed the comfort of complacency and embrace the invigorating challenge of growth. It begins with a clear-eyed assessment of our current state. How effectively are we deploying our resources, both human and financial, to reach out and invite? Do our calendars, budgets, and volunteer schedules reflect a deliberate focus on welcoming newcomers?

The most potent resource we possess isn't a program or budget, but our own faith. Through prayer, focus, and open hearts, we create fertile ground for the Holy Spirit to work. This isn't about forceful proselytization or empty promises; it's about authentically sharing the light that transforms our lives.

Evangelism, then, isn't a grand stage production; it's the quiet symphony of everyday interactions. It's an invitation to a Sunday service, the open door at a potluck, the genuine warmth offered to a newcomer. It's about creating a church where the light of Christ shines so brightly that others are naturally drawn to its warmth.

Every church needs a well-defined evangelism plan, not a rigid blueprint, but a flexible map guiding our efforts. How will we attract visitors and nurture their curiosity? How can we empower new members to become ambassadors of faith, extending their networks and drawing others towards the joy they've found?

Embracing this mission begins with a deliberate shift in perspective. We must turn our gaze outward, to the faces lit only by the faintest glimmer of hope. Our focus becomes those who lack the familiarity of our hymns, the comfort of our fellowship, and the knowledge of scripture that guides our lives. They are the individuals yearning for connection, searching for meaning, and perhaps hesitant to step into the unfamiliar light of a church.

Growing families don't simply happen; they are nurtured, cultivated, and invited to blossom. So, let us shed the cloak of hesitant hikers and embrace the call to share the joy of our faith. Let us become intentional inviters, drawing new seekers to the vibrant community where faith finds its truest expression.

Let us remember the Great Commission wasn't spoken to a select few, but to every follower of Christ. It's a call to step beyond the familiar, to share the light we hold within, and to build a family church that grows not just in numbers, but in the radiance of its shared faith.

Charting the Course - Embracing the Compass of Measurement

Imagine a ship traversing vast oceans, its sails billowing with hope, its destination a distant but cherished dream. Yet, weeks into the voyage, a creeping unease settles over the crew. The captain, his usual confidence shaken, consults his instruments, only to find them faulty, their dials offering nothing but blank stares. Lost amidst the boundless waves, the journey becomes a desperate gamble, driven by guesswork and fervent prayers.

This, in essence, is the plight of a church devoid of measurement. Without reliable instruments, how can we navigate the currents of growth and progress? How can we ensure our efforts steer us towards the shores of vibrant community and spiritual fulfillment?

The family church, while steeped in the warmth of personal connections, cannot dispense with the guiding hand of data. Measurement isn't a cold intrusion into the realm of fellowship; it's a compass, offering crucial insights into the effectiveness of our endeavors. Like attentive gardeners, we must nurture the seeds of faith, but first, we must know where to sow them.

Attendance counts aren't mere numbers; they tell a story of engagement, revealing which programs resonate with our community. Tracking new members isn't about boasting; it helps us identify effective outreach strategies and nurture those taking their first steps on the path of faith. Following up with absent faces isn't an intrusion; it's a bridge, reconnecting those who might have lost their way in the bustling tides of life.

These metrics, carefully gathered and analyzed, become fuel for improvement. We learn which initiatives bear fruit, which ones wither, and which require careful pruning. We experiment, adjusting course as needed, guided by the constant feedback of data. This isn't a rigid roadmap, but a dynamic chart, evolving with the needs and aspirations of our community.

Measurement isn't just about counting heads; it's about understanding hearts. Analyzing visitor demographics gives us a clearer picture of who we're reaching, allowing us to tailor programs and ministries to better serve their needs. Tracking engagement in small groups tells us where conversations spark and connections deepen, guiding us in nurturing these fertile grounds of fellowship.

Setting goals isn't a cold calculation; it's a declaration of aspiration. By establishing clear objectives for our resources, activities, and ministries, we chart a course, aligning our efforts with the desired destination. As we measure progress towards these goals, week by week, month by month, we make informed adjustments, celebrating successes and refining strategies for those falling short.

This isn't about worshipping numbers at the expense of personal connections. It's about using data as a tool, a servant to our mission, not its master. Measurement allows us to focus on our strengths, those initiatives that truly shine and draw life into our community. It frees us from unproductive endeavors, enabling us to reallocate resources towards initiatives with greater potential.

Ultimately, measurement isn't about boasting or control; it's about stewardship. It's about understanding the impact of our efforts, ensuring that every resource, every moment of service, every act of kindness finds its fertile ground, bears fruit, and contributes to the growth of our shared faith.

By embracing the compass of measurement, we sail with confidence, our destination clear, our course constantly refined. We become a church in motion, not adrift in the vast ocean of possibility, but navigating a deliberate course towards the vibrant shores of a thriving family church, where faith finds sanctuary, fellowship thrives, and every soul feels the gentle pull of a welcoming haven.

CONCLUSION: WALKING THE EMMAUS ROAD – BUILDING A FAMILY CHURCH WITH CHRIST

Building a family church isn't a solo endeavor; it's a symphony played by many instruments, a shared journey where every step counts. The path may be winding, the terrain uncharted, but fear not! For many travelers have gone before us. We have ten guiding lights, ten insights gleaned from experience and the scriptures to illuminate the road ahead. Yes, fear may induce its doubts, but like seasoned travelers embarking on ancient dusty paths, guided by flickering oil lamps and tales of distant destinations, we too embark on this journey with courage ignited.

Can you feel the sun already warming your shoulders? Can you hear the anticipation crackling in the air like dry leaves? Take a breath, close your eyes, and let the anticipation of promise carry you back in time.

Imagine a dusty road snaking through sun-drenched hills, two figures trudging in its embrace. Cleopas and another disciple, hearts heavy with disappointment, discuss the shattered dream of Jerusalem. Suddenly, a stranger joins their steps, his gentle voice drawing them into conversation. Unseen, a spark ignites within their souls, fueled by his words that open the scriptures like hidden gardens. As they walk, hope rekindles, doubt crumbles, and understanding dawns. They reach Emmaus, but with newfound yearning, invite the stranger to stay. And in the breaking of bread, their eyes are opened, hearts ablaze with recognition. It is Jesus, alive!

This journey on the Emmaus Road mirrors the path of building a family church. We, too, walk hand-in-hand, not always clear of the way, sometimes burdened by discouragement. But amidst our uncertainties, Christ joins our stride, his presence unseen yet undeniable. We gather weekly, drawn by the promise of his presence. Our fellowship, fueled by shared faith and love, becomes the fertile soil where seeds of hope blossom. We engage in open discussions, wrestle with scripture, and seek His wisdom in all things. In this shared pilgrimage, we are not mere tourists passing through; we are active participants, walking shoulder-to-shoulder with Christ, echoing Cleopas's plea: *"Stay with us."*

And He does. Not just in the sanctuary's embrace, but in the laughter of children during potlucks, in the comfort offered to a grieving soul, in the act of kindness reaching beyond the church walls. His presence permeates our very core, reminding us that even in the ordinary, the divine dwells. Just as Emmaus wasn't the destination, this church we build isn't just about bricks and mortar. It's about hearts awakened, lives transformed, and communities thriving under the sunlit banner of his love.

The road ahead may still have its curves and shadows, but we walk not in fear, but in the light of the revelation received. We carry the embers of hope ignited on the Emmaus Road. We walk on, dear brothers and sisters, holding strong to the flame of faith, and allowing Christ to guide our every step. So, let us walk on, with hearts ablaze, building a church worthy of His presence, a haven of love, and a testament to the transformative power of walking the Emmaus Road, hand in hand with Christ. As we do, we might just hear, amidst the sound of the wind, the gentle echo of His invitation: *"Come, follow me."*

"The long-term pastor, the church's founder, had been unexpectedly moved on. Though a shroud of confusion and anger clouded the details, one thing was clear: the people were hurting."

CHAPTER FIVE

CASE STUDY
A Family Church Blossoms in a Mega-Church Era

A BUMPY START

Fourteen years ago, when I arrived at Christ our Redeemer, I encountered a church in crisis. What had been a strong and vibrant ministry since its founding was teetering on the brink of collapse. This wasn't the result of wrongdoing but the aftermath of a painful separation, akin to a marital dissolution. The long-term pastor, the church's founder, had been unexpectedly moved on. Though a shroud of confusion and anger clouded the details, one thing was clear: *the people were hurting.*

Following this beloved and long-serving leader might have been the prudent path. However, during the interim period, another pastor came and stayed for a mere two weeks. This deepened the wound. It wasn't just the loss of a friend, leader, and familiar face; it was the sting of rejection. To be abandoned after this much investment, after overcoming adversity and establishing themselves within the community, was a bitter pill to swallow.

Adding to the shock was the news that the church was financially strapped. Despite past generosity and successful ministry, they were running on fumes. The internal turmoil led to conflict, departures of key members, and a desperate struggle to keep the doors open. The needs of the facility itself, ever-present in any church, compounded the challenges.

Further complicating matters, I was an outsider brought in from beyond the conference and district. Unaware of their hardships, I arrived at a crossroads with a congregation reeling from loss and uncertainty. Though the opportunity presented itself to reassign me elsewhere, I felt called to stay. The thought of this faithful community suffering another abandonment in such a short time fueled my resolve. So, I committed myself to mending their hearts, minds, and souls.

Those early days were indeed difficult, but also a period of immense personal and spiritual growth. I commuted every weekend from Huntsville, Alabama, with my young children, a seven hour each way journey for four years. This commitment forced me to hone my preaching and deepen my understanding of what truly makes a church *"church."*

There was an unspoken undercurrent at Christ our Redeemer. They would talk about being a loving church, about the strong youth ministry and dedicated elders, but they couldn't quite articulate what it meant. They reminisced about past members and a more vibrant era, hinting at a yearning for something intangible.

As I examined the various programs and ministries, I saw potential for growth but also recognized a breadth that stretched the church's resources thin. Yet, amidst the programs, a few stood out like the monthly birthday cards and senior medicine contributions. These seemingly simple programs resonated with something deeper, a desire for connection and care. Initially, I overlooked their significance too, but upon reflection, something began to crystallize. It wasn't the flashy programs that were the lifeblood of this church, but the quiet gestures of love and support.

In its early days, Christ our Redeemer thrived under the founding pastor's masterful balancing act. He wove together the warmth of a family church with the welcoming arms of a commuter haven, satisfying both desires through diverse programs and an inclusive spirit. It was a perfect recipe for success at the time. However, when I arrived years later, the landscape had shifted dramatically. Mega-churches, like imposing fortresses, had sprouted up around us, casting long shadows across the community. Smaller churches, desperate to echo their grandeur, mimicked the spectacle.

Faced with this evolving terrain, I made a bold choice: we would not chase trends or build a mini megalopolis. We would double down on what made us true – *a sanctuary of family, where faith intertwined with kinship*. It was a risky move, perhaps even foolish in the face of such overwhelming grandeur. Yet, as families blossomed, children found new friends, and seniors reveled in renewed belonging, my conviction only strengthened. Choosing the path of a family church wasn't easy, but the rewards were immeasurable.

BUILDING THE FAMILY CHURCH

Once I grasped the identity and desires of the church, the path ahead became clear. The hardship of my early ministry began to fade. We paid off the mortgage, stabilized membership, and focused on the ministries that would shape our future. My vision was clear: *a church built on faith, family, and fellowship.*

We implemented weekly attendance tracking, followed up with absent members, and structured the calendar around events fostering connection. We consolidated programs to encourage shared activities and eliminated isolated afternoon programs, making worship service the hub of celebrating ministries and holding annual *"days."*

Youth programs became family affairs, incorporating Bible study with praise dancing, African drumming, and music tutoring. Every open door was an invitation to fellowship. We reduced standalone programs, opting for combined offerings to maximize participation. Slowly, through trial and error, we refined our approach, prioritizing fellowship not just on Sundays, but throughout the entire week. Birthdays, anniversaries, and holidays became communal celebrations, transforming the church into a haven for families to grow together spiritually and find like-minded friends.

Building and maintaining a family church was arduous but incredibly rewarding. Walking into Sunday morning and seeing believers of all ages, eager and excited to be in God's house, brought immense joy. This place wasn't just about attending services; it was about inviting friends and experiencing a vibrant spiritual and social community.

We embraced faith and understood family to a degree, but fellowship was often undervalued. The need to connect with those who care, to be accepted and loved, to find joy in the company of like-minded individuals – this is an essential element of Christian faith. It's how we find mentors, support, and strength to navigate life's journey. The church must be a space where believers connect and cultivate meaningful relationships.

Those who drifted away in the early days were mourned, but many more arrived. While I lament those who found their paths elsewhere, I believe every believer seeks something specific, and a church specializing in one niche might not cater to all needs. For those seeking the commuter experience, soaring worship, or hurried connections, other churches exist within the community. They fill their unique niche. However, for those yearning for the warmth and intimacy of a family church, Christ our Redeemer became a haven. We weren't striving to be ubiquitous or trendy; we embraced our distinct calling.

Building a family church wasn't without challenges. Some questioned our focus, yearning for past programs or grander productions. Some felt the shift too drastic, missing the anonymity of a larger congregation. But amidst the anxieties, a quiet transformation unfolded. Warmth filled the air as families flourished, children discovered new friendships, and seniors embraced a renewed sense of community. The church walls buzzed with life, not just on Sundays, but throughout the week. Laughter echoed from game nights, support circles offered solace, and shared meals fostered deep connections.

In a world often characterized by loneliness and isolation, we offer a beacon of hope, a reminder that belonging, acceptance, and love are cornerstones of the Christian faith. Christ our Redeemer may not be the grandest cathedral, but within its walls, a living testimony unfolds. We are a testament to the power of faith, the nurturing embrace of family, and the transformative energy of genuine fellowship.

CHAPTER SIX

TRANSFORMATIONAL SERMONS
More Than Memories:
Rekindling the Family Church Vision

Leviticus 6:8-13 (NLT)

⁸ Then the LORD said to Moses,
⁹ "Give Aaron and his sons the following instructions regarding the burnt offering. The burnt offering must be left on top of the altar until the next morning, and the fire on the altar must be kept burning all night.
¹⁰ In the morning, after the priest on duty has put on his official linen clothing and linen undergarments, he must clean out the ashes of the burnt offering and put them beside the altar.
¹¹ Then he must take off these garments, change back into his regular

clothes, and carry the ashes outside the camp to a place that is ceremonially clean.

12 Meanwhile, the fire on the altar must be kept burning; it must never go out. Each morning the priest will add fresh wood to the fire and arrange the burnt offering on it. He will then burn the fat of the peace offerings on it.

13 Remember, the fire must be kept burning on the altar at all times. It must never go out.

INTRODUCTION

The Day of Pentecost was a fiery baptism, the Holy Spirit descending upon the church like tongues of flame. This image resonated deeply with the Jewish people, for throughout their history, fire had been a potent symbol of God's power and presence. They had witnessed it flicker in the burning bush that spoke to Moses, rise like smoke from the fiery summit of Mount Sinai, and guide them through the wilderness as a pillar of light. They had seen Elijah command fire from heaven to vanquish the prophets of Baal, and witnessed its miraculous descent to consume the temple offering upon its completion.

This was the fire that the temple priests meticulously nurtured, ensuring its perpetual blaze through the night to prepare for the morning sacrifice. It was a living symbol of God's ceaseless presence amidst His people. And now, that same fire burns not just in stone temples, but within the very hearts of every Christian.

The care and attentiveness with which the priests tended the temple fire offers a lesson for us all. We, too, must nurture the spiritual fire that fuels our ministry and imbues our actions with holy power. We must be wary of churches where the embers have lost their glow, where choirs lack fervor and pews sit tepid. I've seen those churches, felt the chilling absence of passion, and as a pastor, I know the temptation to simply walk away.

But fire is a force that ignites, that compels us to run with an unseen wind at our backs, dance to an unheard rhythm, and raise our voices when silence reigns. It's the spark that propels us to choose right when tempted to stray, the force that crackles within us when the Holy Spirit takes hold. It's like fire shut up in our bones, a consuming energy that drives us to serve, to love, and to share the unwavering light of faith.

This is the fire we must tend, fanning its flames and ensuring its radiance. And it all starts with remembering, with actively stoking the embers within us so that their glow may illuminate the world around us.

❖ POINT 1: WORKING THE FIRE

The temple priest wasn't just a fire starter; he was a fire artist. Once the evening sacrifice blazed, his job became a delicate dance of maintaining the flames without adding more fuel. He'd fan the embers, gently coaxing them to lick higher, and expertly stir the coals, ensuring even heat throughout. This intricate process held a profound lesson: sometimes, the solution to our problems isn't more resources, but working with what we have, igniting the existing passion and enthusiasm.

I used to think a church needed more people, more money, a bigger building to truly thrive. But then I understood the priest's quiet power. Without fanfare, he kept the fire alive, and in its warmth, everything blossomed. Passion? It's the fuel that makes the impossible seem possible. Witnessing it was like hearing the same story of Jesus' sacrifice every Sunday, but through fresh eyes. Each preacher, in their own way, fanned the flames, reminding us of the transformative power within the fire – the power to save, heal, forgive, and bless.

This truth resonates beyond the pulpit. The hymns we sing, the stories we share, the acts of kindness we perform – all these are embers we tend, waiting for the moment they erupt into blazing love for Jesus and His grace. People don't crave endless fundraisers; they hunger for the embers of faith to be fanned, for reminders that they met the Man from Galilee, that the balm of Gilead still soothes, and that Jesus' love remains the one constant friend in this ever-changing world.

- I love to tell the story
  Of unseen things above
  Of Jesus and his glory
  Of Jesus and his love.

- I love to tell the story
  Because I know 'tis true
  It satisfies my longings
  As nothing else can do.

❖ Point 2: Take out the Ashes

The temple fire demanded not just tending, but cleaning. The priest's duty wasn't merely to keep the flames dancing, but to clear the altar of ashes, ensuring they didn't smother the life-giving blaze. This carries a profound lesson for us: we too must learn to navigate the delicate dance between respecting the past and embracing renewal.

Yesterday's victories, like treasured ashes, deserve reverence. But clinging to them can't fuel today's fire. We must find the sacred balance, the sweet spot where past wisdom informs our journey without becoming fossilized burdens. Sometimes, our attachment to the ashes can choke the present, like the boy mourning his goldfish, unable to move on and let new life bloom.

I am reminded of a man in the back yard one day. As he peered over his fence and spotted his neighbor's little boy digging a hole in the backyard, tears streaming down his face with each shovelful. Concerned, the man called out, *"What are you doing there, young man?"* The boy sniffled, *"My goldfish died, the one I loved dearly, and I'm burying him."* The man chuckled, *"That's an awfully big hole for a goldfish, isn't it?"* The boy wiped his eyes, patted down the final mound of dirt, and declared, *"That's because he's still inside your cat!"*

This can happen when churches become museums of past glories, clinging to outdated methods instead of adapting to the ever-changing needs of a new generation. Jesus himself said, *"No one puts new wine into old wineskins; otherwise, the wineskins burst, and the wine is spilled, and the wineskins are ruined. But new wine must be put into new wineskins."*

Letting go of the ashes doesn't mean forgetting history; it means understanding that God isn't confined to yesterday's embers. He is the ever-flowing fire, constantly evolving, blazing with boundless potential. Programs, music, technology – these are mere vessels, and like the wineskins, they must adjust to accommodate the ever-fresh outpouring of His grace.

People don't come to church seeking yesterday's ashes; they crave the warmth of the living fire. They yearn to know that the Lord remains a healer, a savior, a miracle worker, a shelter in the storm. They come to feel the presence of that *"wheel in the midst of a wheel,"* that unyielding rock in a weary land.

So, let us be wise stewards of the fire, respecting the embers of the past while fanning the flames of the future. Let us embrace the dynamism of faith, knowing that God's story isn't confined to dusty pages but unfolds with each new sunrise, each whispered prayer, each act of love. We are not caretakers of a museum; we are stokers of a fire, and its radiance depends on our willingness to embrace both the ashes and the flames.

Conclusion: Stir It

We all know the sting of a disappointing conference, the hollow echoes of empty pews, and the whispered anxieties that creep in when the only faces filling the church are the same unwavering few. We travel miles, invest hope, and pour prayers into building a flame, only to sometimes feel like it's sputtering its last. What then, when doubts whisper about the church's future, when Sunday mornings turn into a monotonous parade of familiarity, and passion seems almost gone?

I am reminded of a little boy who'd been begging his dad for a camping trip for years. But Dad was always traveling, never having time.

Then, one Saturday morning, Dad's boss called about a scheduling mistake — he had the weekend off! It was ecstasy, not just for the break, but because it was the boy's birthday. So, they packed the car, the boy's whoops echoing through the air, and they were off to the campsite.

They fished, hunted, and collected rocks. At night, they sat around the crackling campfire, stories weaving between them like smoke, marshmallows melting into gooey perfection.

Morning arrived too soon, the fading embers carrying a bittersweet scent. The boy, heart heavy with the thought of leaving, wandered to the campfire's remains. In a silent outburst of melancholy, he began flinging his collected treasures, rock by rock. One sharp stone, misdirected by grief, ricocheted off a charred log. Bark exploded, revealing a vibrant heart of fire beneath. Sizzling embers scattered, and the boy stumbled back, startled by the sudden heat. His Dad's voice, sharp with concern, cut through the air: *"Be careful!"*

It looks like the fire is out, but if you stir it, it will burn again.

When the flames flicker and doubts arise, remember this: Preach Jesus. Preach his miracles, not as dusty lore, but as embers ready to blaze. Preach his parables, not as riddles to solve, but as windows to His grace.

Preach his transfiguration, not as a spectacle, but as a glimpse of glory to come. Preach his crucifixion, not as morbid tale, but as the bridge to boundless love. Preach his resurrection, not as distant echo, but as hope that conquers darkness. Preach his ascension, not as farewell, but as promise: He walks with us still. When you have preached all this start over again. Stir the fire, friends. Work the embers, fan the flames.

For when we preach Jesus, not as fading memory, but as ever-present light, the fire within us, and within our churches, will never truly die. It will crackle, it will dance, it will illuminate the path forward, generation after generation.

"When the flames flicker and doubts arise, remember this: Preach Jesus. Preach his miracles, not as dusty lore, but as embers ready to blaze. Preach his parables, not as riddles to solve, but as windows to His grace."

2 Kings 4:2-5 (NLT)
² "What can I do to help you?" Elisha asked. "Tell me, what do you have in the house?" "Nothing at all, except a flask of olive oil," she replied.
³ And Elisha said, "Borrow as many empty jars as you can from your friends and neighbors.
⁴ Then go into your house with your sons and shut the door behind you. Pour olive oil from your flask into the jars, setting each one aside when it is filled."
⁵ So she did as she was told. Her sons kept bringing jars to her, and she filled one after another.

INTRODUCTION

After a holiday feast or any big celebration, you know what I love? Leftovers. Those last bits of the good stuff, sitting there on the plate. But sometimes, there's just enough to make you miss the party all over again, without quite filling you up. Those scattered bites spark nostalgia, like faded photographs of happy faces around the table. But their dwindling portions hold a hint of melancholy, a reminder that the party's over and the plates soon empty.

This widow, facing debt and the threat of losing her sons, approached Elisha in tears. Her story resonates with many of us. We, too, have felt the sting of scarcity, the nagging worry that our once-sufficient resources just don't stretch far enough. We see it in the fading grandeur of old churches, the echoes of hymns sung by larger choirs, the empty pews where vibrant faith once flourished. Memories of a fuller past remind us of what is missing, leaving us to wonder, *"How did we end up here?"*

But fear not friends! Our scripture offers a beacon of hope in the midst of *leftovers*. Through the widow's story, we discover a path to not just survive, but thrive, even when living on what remains. This is not simply about scraping by and making do; it's about a radical transformation, a multiplication of faith that turns scarcity into abundance. So, let us open our hearts to the wisdom of this ancient tale and discover how, even with seemingly empty flasks, we can fill our lives, and our churches, with a wellspring of hope and renewal.

❖ Point 1: Survey the House

Facing down a mountain of debt and the looming threat of losing her sons, the widow stood before Elisha, her spirit as crumpled as the clothes clinging to her frame. Tears blurred the world, and despair whispered its suffocating song in her ear. *"What can I do?"* she cried: her voice raw with helplessness. *"Nothing,"* she sighed, the word heavy like a stone settling in her stomach.

But Elisha, with the gentle wisdom of a prophet who'd seen the ebb and flow of life's tides, wouldn't let her answer stand. *"Tell me,"* he asked, his gaze unwavering yet kind, *"what do you have in your house, anything at all?"*

In this wasteland of fear and loss, could there possibly be anything left? She cast her mind back, sifting through the wreckage of her shattered world. Then, a faint memory flickered, as fragile as a butterfly wing. *"Just a flask of oil."*

It was little, barely enough for one final anointing, a meager echo of her husband's ministry now silenced. Yet, in that humble flask, a spark of hope refused to be extinguished. For even in the ashes of tragedy, God speaking blessings, waiting to be discovered, like treasures buried beneath the rubble. Shifting our focus from lack to abundance unlocks a world of possibilities. Focusing on what we lack blinds us to God's blessings. I recall a conversation between a husband and wife during their hard times.

> Wife: *"I'm ashamed of the way we live,"* she said to her lazy husband who wouldn't get a job. *"My father pays our rent, my mother buys all of our food, my sister buys our clothes, my aunt bought us a car. I'm just so ashamed."* Husband: *"You should be ashamed,"* he said. *"Those two worthless brothers of yours never give us anything!"*

Life has a funny way of making us fixate on what we lack, causing us to overlook the blessings right under our noses. We might yearn for fancy cars and diamond rings, but forget the warmth of the roof over our heads and the comfort of a full belly. Mama used to say, *"Child, you can cry about the hole in your shoe, or you can dance in the sunshine it lets in."* It's all about perspective, isn't it?

Remember that old church on the hilltop? They couldn't afford a fancy organ, so the carpenter's son beat out a rhythm on a washboard while Mama Mary's hum filled the air. The blacksmith built the pews with his own sweat, and the farmers brought their harvest to fill the cupboards. They had little, but they made it work, fueled by faith and community. They knew true abundance wasn't about wealth, but about the bonds they shared, the work they did, and the simple joy of a shared meal.

❖ Point 2: Shut the Door

Just like the prophet instructed the widow to gather her vessels and shut the door, sometimes the Lord works in quiet, requiring us to close out the din of the world. There's a time for open arms and vibrant conversation, but when God paints His path on our hearts, when He sets our steps on a new journey, it's crucial to slam the door on negativity.

Oh, we can hear them already, the naysayers and gossips, their voices sharp and cutting like rusted blades. *"Why borrow all those pots? You haven't got a morsel to fill them!"* they sneer. *"No money? Leave that crazy prophet alone! Your poor husband, worn out chasing shadows of salvation!"* Their doubts dance a jig on our insecurities, their skepticism a poison seeping into our faith.

But listen closely, for in the hush of closed doors, God often plants the seeds of His greatest miracles. He lets us reach the edge of desperation, strips away the distractions, until we finally stop caring who sees us weep and what they whisper behind cupped hands. It's in that raw vulnerability, when we're down to our very last drop of hope, that we finally turn our weary eyes heavenward and rasp, *"God, it's all yours."*

Oh, believe it, for when we're down to nothing, God is up to something. He's the potter who molds us in the quiet kiln of solitude, crafting vessels of purpose from the clay of our brokenness. He's the alchemist who turns our tears into liquid gold, refining our faith in the crucible of doubt.

So, when life throws its punches, when insomnia paints shadows on your ceiling, don't count sheep – talk to the Shepherd.

> Have a little talk with Jesus
> tell Him all about our troubles.
> (He will) hear our fainted cry
> (He will) answer by and by.

Remember, Jesus himself said, *"When you pray, enter into your closet, and when you have shut thy door, pray to your Father who is in the secret place, and your Father who sees in secret will reward you openly."* So close the door on negativity, open your heart to His presence, and watch as He transforms your emptiness into a vessel overflowing with His grace.

CLOSE: HOW BIG IS YOUR FAITH?

Always remember the widow, clutching the prophet's word, her mind likely swirling with questions. Why borrow so many pots when her cupboard gaped empty? Everyone knew her plight, the bitterness of debt clinging to her like a shroud. Yet, she obeyed, faith a whispered ember in her heart.

Oh, if she'd held back, borrowed just a few vessels, her blessing would have been a meager trickle. But she cast doubt aside, embracing possibility. And as the oil flowed, surpassing the rim of each borrowed pot, her faith erupted into a roaring flame. *"Fill that vase!"* she cried, *"Bring every mug, every jar, every basin!"* Her trust painted the room with a golden tide, each vessel overflowing, a testament to her unwavering belief.

In the end, that widow not only drowned her debts, but lived a life nourished by the oil's bounty. God, you see, doesn't just fill our needs, He turns our leftovers into abundance. He rewards not the size of our possessions, but the magnitude of our faith.

> My son strolled into the living room one day, eyes wide with a question on his mind. *"Dad,"* he asked, *"where's the Tooth Fairy? I left a tooth, but there's no money under my pillow!"* Then, with a glint of suspicion in his gaze, he added, *"Are you the Tooth Fairy?"*

> Caught off guard, I chuckled and explained the protocol. *"You let me know when you lose a tooth, and I'll telegram the Tooth Fairy so she can schedule a visit. Just leave your tooth in a bag under the pillow, and It'll be filled with money in the morning!"*

See, children have this remarkable way of taking things literally, unburdened by cynicism or doubt. So, that night, I tiptoed into his room, expecting a small pouch or maybe a plastic snack bag. But guess what I found? A full-blown garbage bag, housing his lost tooth like a trophy in a display case! You see, when I promised a treasure trove of money, his faith envisioned mountains of it, demanding the biggest container he could find. He didn't hold back, didn't limit himself to small expectations. He believed with his whole heart, and that's the point,

Don't limit God with doubt but embrace the limitless possibilities of His love. Remember, our faith dictates the size of the blessings we receive, so open your hearts wide and watch miracles cascade in, filling your life with an abundance beyond measure.

> I'm looking for a miracle.
> Expect the impossible.
> Feel the intangible.
> See the invisible,
> The sky is the limit to what I can have.

The sky is the limit to what I can have
I believe and receive it,
God will perform today.

"Don't limit God with doubt but embrace the limitless possibilities of His love. Remember, our faith dictates the size of the blessings we receive, so open your hearts wide and watch miracles cascade in, filling your life with an abundance beyond measure."

ABOUT THE AUTHOR

Rev. Dr. Roger A. Richardson, Sr.

Rev. Dr. Roger A. Richardson is the pastor of Christ Our Redeemer AME Church in Blackjack, Missouri where he has served since 2012. He accepted his calling to the ministry at age 12 at his home church, First AME Church, Los Angeles, under the pastoral leadership of Rev. Dr. Cecil "Chip" Murray.

Rev. Dr. Richardson began his academic career at Tuskegee University, earning a Bachelor's degree in Political science. He also attended Alabama A&M University where he earned a Master's degree in Urban & Regional Planning. He is a graduate of Payne Theological Seminary where he received his Master of Divinity. He received a Ph. D in Public Administration from Auburn University.

He holds a certificate in Nonprofit Management from Auburn University Montgomery. Rev. Dr. Richardson holds a certificate in Social Science Research from ICPSR at the University of Michigan. He is also a graduate of the Management Development Program at Harvard University's Graduate School of Higher Education. In academia, he has served as a professor, outreach specialist, research director and program director.

He has served on the faculty of University of Southern Indiana, Kentucky State University, Alabama A&M University, Payne Theological Seminary, and Aldersgate School of Ministry. As a professor, he has taught a wide range of courses dealing with ministry and community development.

Rev. Dr. Richardson draws upon his experience as an educator to equip and educate the saints with the Word of God. The central focus of his ministry is preparing God's people to be Christ's ambassadors to the lost as outlined in II Corinthians 5:20.

Rev. Dr. Richardson has faithfully served as a pastor in the Thirteenth, Ninth and Fifth Episcopal Districts and has provided pastoral leadership for the following congregations:

- Craig Chapel AME Church, Salvisa Kentucky
- St. Paul AME Church, Hurtsboro Alabama
- Emmanuel AME Church, Birmingham Alabama
- St. John AME Church, Graysville Alabama
- Lee Chapel AME Church, Edgewater Alabama
- Christ Our Redeemer AME Church, Black Jack Missouri

He is married to Joi Richardson and they have two children, Naomi and Roger Richardson Jr.

REFLECTIONS

REFLECTIONS

REFLECTIONS

THE FAMILY CHURCH
Faith | Family | Fellowship

"What I like about this book is the invitation to explore the hidden gems in the **Family Church** such as the unique strengths, the transformative power of intimacy, where belonging is not just a word but an actual experience that exists in the **Family Church**."

—Bishop Frederick Alan Wright, Sr.

"We stand on the precipice of a new era. An era where the familiar ground beneath our feet feels like shifting sand. The anchors of community, family, and institutions that once held firm seem to be slowly giving way."

—Rev. Dr. Roger A. Richardson

ISBN 979-8-9863598-4-7

www.ingramcontent.com/pod-product-compliance
Lightning Source LLC
Chambersburg PA
CBHW070517100426
42743CB00010B/1850